THE**BIBLEIN**AMERICA

THE CHANGING LANDSCAPE OF BIBLE PERCEPTIONS AND ENGAGEMENT

A 6-YEAR BARNA STUDY PRODUCED IN PARTNERSHIP WITH AMERICAN BIBLE SOCIETY

CONTENTS

Preface by Jason Malec 5

Introduction by David Kinnaman 7

Part I: The Big Picture of the Bible in America 13

1. What Americans Believe About the Bible 16
2. Bible Engagement in America 20

   Special Report: The Bible & Discipleship 26

3. The Bible in Entertainment 28
4. The Bible in Society & Politics 31
5. Bible-Minded Cities 34

   Special Report: State of the Bible 1816 38

Part II: The Bible in a Changing Context 41

6. Bible Literacy 47
7. The Good Book in a Digital Context 51
8. The Rise of Bible Skeptics 56
9. What Compels or Prevents Engagement? 58

   Special Report: When Life Stops Making Sense 63

Part III: The Bible Among Key Demographics 67

10. Practicing Christians 70
11. Catholics 72

    Q&A with Sir Mario Paredes 75

12. Hispanic Americans 78

    Q&A with Rev. Bonnie Camarda 81

13. African Americans 82

    Q&A with Bishop Claude Alexander 85

Part IV: The Bible for Every Generation 87

14. What Younger Generations Believe 91

    Special Report: Teens & the Bible 97

15. How Younger Generations Engage.................. 101

    Q&A with Rev. Rob Hoskins.................. 113

16. Millennials & the Bible "Brand" 115

17. The Good News 122

    Special Report: The Bible in a
    Post-Christian Context...................... 124

Part V: Deepening Bible Engagement 129

    A Message from Roy Peterson,
    President of American Bible Society........ 135

Appendix

A. Data Tables 139

B. Profiles of Bible Engagement 155

C. Glossary 164

D. Methodology.................................... 167

E. Endnotes 169

Acknowledgements 171

About... 173

PREFACE

By Jason Malec
Managing Director of American Bible Society's Mission U.S.

These are important times.

This phrase has been uttered for centuries, if not millennia. It would be the height of chronological snobbery to assume that our current circumstances are more important than anything in the past. And yet we do seem to be at a unique juncture.

According to some sociologists and historians, major culture changes often take place in 500-year cycles. We can see epic shifts in the realms of transportation, communication, technology, science and faith. These culture changes dramatically affect human existence.

Many experts believe we are smack dab in the middle of one of these transitions. During the last century, they argue, we evolved from "modern" to "postmodern," initiating what many suggest is a new era. *The Jetsons*-style self-driving cars, holographic video meetings, virtual and augmented reality, mind-bending quantum discoveries . . . the list goes on and on, in a dizzying array of so-called innovation and progress.

What about faith? Is faith also evolving with the times, or is there something timeless in transcendent truths that resists all variation? And what about the Bible? Over the course of American history, it has played a central role in shaping nearly every area of society, including art, politics, morality, ethics, science, philosophy and, of course, theology. Without question, it has had a more profound impact on our culture than any other book—but is its influence coming to an end with this latest cycle?

We don't know what the future holds, but surveys can show us where we stand. By asking crucial questions, we can get a picture of the current situation, which we can then compare to snapshots from previous years. This helps us identify trends.

OVER THE COURSE OF AMERICAN HISTORY, FAITH HAS PLAYED A CENTRAL ROLE IN SHAPING NEARLY EVERY AREA OF SOCIETY

This landmark report compiles data Barna researchers have collected and analyzed over the course of six years for what American Bible Society calls the "State of the Bible." There is much to celebrate! At the same time, however, there are some alarming trends. In light of recent history in other Western countries—throughout Europe and Canada, for example—it is sobering to see in America the stark reality of Bible skepticism rising as engagement declines. If the current trends continue, the Bible will certainly lose its place as our leading culture-shaping factor.

What should we do with this information?

A doom-and-gloom outlook won't help. After all, the Author of the Book still speaks powerfully through it. Perhaps the down-trending data will help us improve the way we present the Bible. At least it should inspire us to engage with the Scriptures ourselves and to share that experience with others.

Our hope for *The Bible in America* is to create awareness—of how things are, but also how they *can* be. Inspiration leads to transformation. The Scriptures themselves declare, "All Scripture is inspired by God and is useful for teaching the truth, rebuking error, correcting faults, and giving instruction for right living, so that the person who serves God may be fully qualified and equipped to do every kind of good deed" (2 Tim 3:16–17).

> THE BIBLE REMAINS ONE OF GOD'S MOST IMPORTANT TOOLS TO TRANSFORM AND REDEEM HIS CREATION

These are indeed important times. The good news—and, yes, we're talking about the Good News—is that the Bible remains one of God's most important tools to transform and redeem his creation. Armed with this timeless narrative of cosmic redemption, God's people will continue to embody the life and teachings of Christ, for the good of the world.

We pray you are both inspired and transformed.

INTRODUCTION

By David Kinnaman
President of Barna Group

Sometimes research is like putting the pieces of a puzzle together without a box top. The process itself is the only way for a cohesive picture to emerge, because you don't know ahead of time what the picture is. You may have some idea what you're working on, but you can't see the big picture until each piece falls into place.

Studying the Bible in America is like that.

For more than 30 years, Barna has studied the Bible's role in and influence on American society, painstakingly collecting the pieces of data we need to understand the big picture.

And for the past six years, we have partnered with American Bible Society to add depth and detail to the picture, and to identify how it is changing over time. Since 2011, Barna has conducted more than 14,000 "State of the Bible" interviews with U.S. adults and teens on behalf of American Bible Society. *The Bible in America* represents one of the largest sets of aggregate data our firm has ever collected on any single topic. We have learned much, even as we continue to discover new and better ways of describing the impact of the Scriptures on Americans' hearts, homes and communities.

We believe this is a crucial moment in American life, a pivotal season that requires Christian leaders to understand the times and know what to do (see 1 Chron. 12:32). The Bible witnesses to the unchanging realities of God and his purposes for the world and, at the same time, depicts that world and its people constantly changing, sometimes for the worse and others for the better. Just like God's people in days past, we can trust that ultimately his purposes will prevail—even if it often feels to many people that today's changes are definitely for the worse.

What is so urgent about our time and place?

THE BIBLE IN AMERICA REPRESENTS ONE OF THE LARGEST SETS OF AGGREGATE DATA BARNA HAS EVER COLLECTED ON A SINGLE TOPIC

A New Landscape

Let's start by describing three major changes that are reshaping the landscape in which we read and engage with the Bible. (Of course, there are many trends that impact the Bible's traction in culture, but these three pieces of the puzzle jump out from the data.) As you'll see throughout *The Bible in America*, these shifts are most apparent among today's youngest generations so, in a sense, they give shape to the present and future reality within which we read and interact with the Bible.

1. *Increasing skepticism.* More people have more questions about the origins, relevance and authority of the Scriptures.
2. *A new moral code.* Self-fulfillment has become the cultural measure of what is good, setting up a conflict between society and the Church.
3. *Digital access.* New tools and technologies are making the Bible—and everything else—more accessible than ever before.

Let me briefly tackle each of these here, and we'll come back to them throughout this report.

First, the steady rise of skepticism is creating a cultural atmosphere that is becoming unfriendly—sometimes even hostile—to claims of faith. In a society that venerates science and rationalism, it is an increasingly hard pill to swallow that an eclectic assortment of ancient stories, poems, sermons, prophecies and letters, written and compiled over the course of 3,000 years, is somehow the sacred "word of God." Even in just the few years Barna has been conducting "State of the Bible" interviews, the data is trending toward Bible skepticism. With each passing year, the percent of Americans who believe that the Bible is "just another book written by men" increases. So too does the perception that the Bible is actually harmful and that people who live by its principles are religious extremists.

THE STEADY RISE OF SKEPTICISM IS CREATING A CULTURAL ATMOSPHERE THAT IS UNFRIENDLY—SOMETIMES EVEN HOSTILE—TO CLAIMS OF FAITH

The Bible in America offers an in-depth examination of these sobering data. Of course, a healthy dose of skepticism means that people are still asking questions of faith, of Christianity and of the Bible. We believe those questions, when asked and answered honestly and from a biblical point of view, can lead to the Spirit's work in people's lives.

Second, as Gabe Lyons and I propose in *Good Faith*, the broader culture has adopted *self-fulfillment* as its ultimate measure of moral good. The shift that is underway moves authority from outside ourselves (for example, the Bible) to within us. This is why so many in our culture talk about identity and "finding themselves"; it is becoming rarer to find people who discover the truest thing about themselves is their identity in Jesus.[1] Increasingly, Americans are rejecting external sources of moral authority, both spiritual and civic. Instead, the Self has become the spiritual and moral compass for the vast majority of adults. Our research highlights the extent to which Americans pledge allegiance to the moral code of self-fulfillment, summed up in six guiding principles. (See table on the following page.)

In stark contrast to the people (including far too many Christians) who embrace self-fulfillment as the highest good, the Bible teaches that God's moral order leads to human and societal flourishing. And the more Christians are oriented toward the way of life described by the Scriptures, the more likely it becomes that they will come into conflict with the dominant culture. As the data shows, fidelity to the Scriptures remains high among practicing Christians, including young adults—but for many, faithfulness comes at real social cost. How can the Christian community help disciples of all ages remain faithful as the culture becomes more intolerant?

Third, the explosive growth of digital tools such as Bible apps, daily reading plans, study resources and online communities offer unprecedented access to the Scriptures. In one recent 28-day period, according to YouVersion's engagement data, people in just the United States used the mobile app to access translations in 554 languages and to request more than *half a billion* chapters

FIDELITY TO THE SCRIPTURES REMAINS HIGH AMONG PRACTICING CHRISTIANS, INCLUDING YOUNG ADULTS—BUT FAITHFULNESS COMES AT REAL SOCIAL COST

THE NEW MORAL CODE

Please indicate whether you agree or disagree with each of the following statements.

% completely + somewhat agree

	% ALL ADULTS	% PRACTICING CHRISTIANS
The best way to find yourself is by looking within yourself	91	76
People should not criticize someone else's life choices	89	76
To be fulfilled in life, you should pursue the things you desire most	86	72
The highest goal of life is to enjoy it as much as possible	84	67
People can believe whatever they want, as long as those beliefs don't affect society	79	61
Any kind of sexual expression between two consenting adult is acceptable	69	40

Barna OmniPoll, August 2015, N=1,000 / Source: Good Faith, 2016

of the Bible.[2] These tools are an incredible leap forward in the "Bible cause" of giving every person on earth access to God's word in his or her own language. What a privilege to partner with the Holy Spirit during this all-access revolution.

At the same time, digital access also means an unfiltered flood of ideas and information that must be evaluated for goodness and truth. An Internet browser is a gateway to an untold vastness of information, but can it also be a pathway for the soul to be shaped in the way of Jesus? The need for godly discernment and rich, relational discipleship has never been greater. Are we equipping disciples, especially *young* disciples, with the spiritual, emotional and mental tools they need to live wisely and for God's glory in the "screen age"?

The report you hold evaluates a robust set of data in light of these three trends.

Windows of Opportunity

To understand the times and know what to do, Christian leaders need a complete picture—not just the edge pieces of the puzzle. And, thankfully, the data is not all bad news. In fact, Barna researchers continue to find bright pieces to the puzzle that demonstrate the Bible's cultural staying power and persistent hold on people's hearts.

- Most Americans (including a majority of young adults) believe the Bible has been more influential on humanity than any other text.
- A majority (also including young adults) believes the Bible contains everything a person needs to know in order to live a meaningful life.
- Two-thirds of all Americans hold an orthodox view of the Bible, that it is the actual or inspired word of God.
- Nearly half read the Scriptures at least once a month.
- Fidelity to the Bible is strong among practicing Christians of all ages.
- As America culture becomes more post-Christian—that is, as the population moves away from Christian beliefs and practices—there is some evidence that interest in the Bible may be on the rise.

TWO-THIRDS OF ALL AMERICANS HOLD AN ORTHODOX VIEW OF THE BIBLE, THAT IT IS THE ACTUAL OR INSPIRED WORD OF GOD

Each of these realities, among others, is a window of opportunity open to leaders. But these windows are not likely to remain open forever, so we must take full advantage to advocate today for the Bible in our skeptical, self-centered, highly connected world.

We should not ignore or minimize the stiffening headwinds. The world is becoming less faith-friendly, but God has given us the astonishing task of trying to keep up with his work. "Do you not perceive it?" (see Is. 43:19). Culturally speaking, the pace of life continues to speed up. The accelerated, frenzied day-to-day living of millions leaves them wanting deeper answers. The Bible can be, as it always has been, a signpost to and conduit of the Word of God made flesh in Jesus Christ.

The Bible is the puzzle piece without which a picture of lasting faith is incomplete. The more data we collect, the more evidence we find that a person's view of and approach to the Bible is a key indicator of Christian faith that lasts. For example, a young person is more likely to continue in her faith commitment if she is engaged with the Bible than if she is active in a local church. This is not to say that connection to a community of faith is unimportant—far from it. But lasting faith is more strongly correlated to engagement with the Scriptures.

Part I paints with a broad brush to sketch a picture of the Bible's place in various sectors of American life. Part II zooms in on the trends Barna has uncovered through six years of "State of the Bible" research. Part III takes a closer look at various demographic categories, such as practicing Christians and Hispanic Americans, to understand how groups differ from each other. Part IV examines generational differences, both among the general U.S. population of teens and adults and among practicing Christians. And finally, Part V offers 10 insights that will help you apply these findings to your own context.

With that, we invite you into *The Bible in America*.

THE MORE DATA WE COLLECT, THE MORE EVIDENCE WE FIND THAT A PERSON'S VIEW OF AND APPROACH TO THE BIBLE IS A KEY INDICATOR OF CHRISTIAN FAITH THAT LASTS

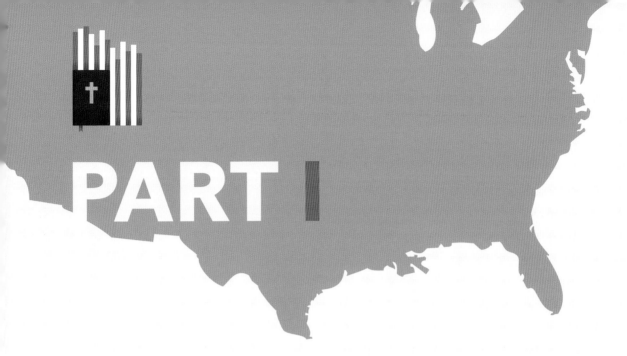

PART I

THE BIG PICTURE OF THE BIBLE IN AMERICA

What do Americans believe about the Bible? How acquainted are they with its stories, principles and message? Do they see the Scriptures as authoritative for society, for their church and family, or personally for themselves? And if so, how often do they actually read the Bible—and how deeply do they consider what it means for their life?

To understand the landscape of Bible beliefs and engagement in the United States, Barna researchers aggregated more than 12,000 "State of the Bible" interviews with U.S. adults into a single database. Part I is the 30,000-foot view of the Bible in America, a survey of what role the Scriptures play in people's lives. We'll look at data for the general U.S. population, and at the Bible's impact on various sectors of U.S. society.

The big picture? Americans hold the Bible in high regard.

But not every part of the picture is saturated with the same shade of belief.

TRACKING THE INFLUENCE OF THE BIBLE

For more than 30 years, Barna has been tracking Americans' beliefs and behaviors related to the Bible.

For the last six years, Barna has powered the American Bible Society's State of the Bible research.

Highlights of the research findings in each of those years.

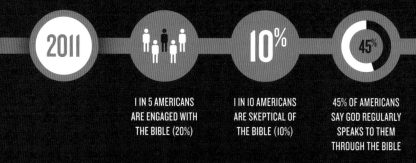

2011

I IN 5 AMERICANS ARE ENGAGED WITH THE BIBLE (20%)

10%

I IN IO AMERICANS ARE SKEPTICAL OF THE BIBLE (10%)

45%

45% OF AMERICANS SAY GOD REGULARLY SPEAKS TO THEM THROUGH THE BIBLE

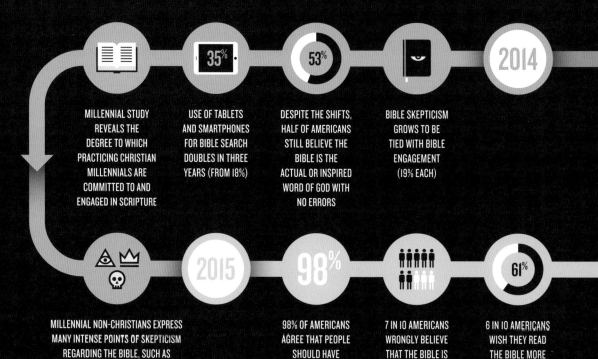

MILLENNIAL STUDY REVEALS THE DEGREE TO WHICH PRACTICING CHRISTIAN MILLENNIALS ARE COMMITTED TO AND ENGAGED IN SCRIPTURE

35%

USE OF TABLETS AND SMARTPHONES FOR BIBLE SEARCH DOUBLES IN THREE YEARS (FROM 18%)

53%

DESPITE THE SHIFTS, HALF OF AMERICANS STILL BELIEVE THE BIBLE IS THE ACTUAL OR INSPIRED WORD OF GOD WITH NO ERRORS

BIBLE SKEPTICISM GROWS TO BE TIED WITH BIBLE ENGAGEMENT (19% EACH)

2014

MILLENNIAL NON-CHRISTIANS EXPRESS MANY INTENSE POINTS OF SKEPTICISM REGARDING THE BIBLE, SUCH AS PERCEPTIONS THAT IT IS MERELY MYTHOLOGY (38%), A FAIRY TALE (30%) AND DANGEROUS (27%)

2015

98%

98% OF AMERICANS AGREE THAT PEOPLE SHOULD HAVE ACCESS TO THE BIBLE

7 IN IO AMERICANS WRONGLY BELIEVE THAT THE BIBLE IS AVAILABLE IN ALL LANGUAGES

61%

6 IN IO AMERICANS WISH THEY READ THE BIBLE MORE

2012

AMERICANS REVEAL A
STRANGE MIX OF HUMILITY
AND OVER-CONFIDENCE
ABOUT THEIR KNOWLEDGE
OF THE BIBLE

69% OF ADULTS
CELEBRATE
EASTER AS A
RELIGIOUS HOLIDAY
HONORING JESUS'
RESURRECTION

55% OF ADULTS
AGREE THAT THE
BIBLE TEACHES THAT
PEOPLE SHOULD PRAY
FOR GOVERNMENT
LEADERS

46% OF ADULTS
CORRECTLY IDENTIFIED
(FROM A LIST OF
OPTIONS) THE FIRST
FIVE BOOKS OF THE
BIBLE

2013

7 IN 10 VIEWERS OF
THE BIBLE MINISERIES
SAY THE PROGRAM
GAVE THEM A
"SURPRISE OR NEW
DISCOVERY" ABOUT
THE BIBLE

1 IN 7 AMERICANS
VIEWED SOME
PORTION OF *THE BIBLE*
MINISERIES, PRODUCED
BY MARK BURNETT AND
ROMA DOWNEY, ON THE
HISTORY CHANNEL

PEOPLE INCREASINGLY
LOOK TO THE BIBLE
TO FIND ANSWERS TO
LIFE'S QUESTIONS
(UP FROM 26% IN 2011)

MORE THAN HALF
COME TO THE BIBLE
TO FIND INTIMACY
WITH GOD

2016

THE GROUP OF BIBLE
SKEPTICS HAS GROWN
TO 1 IN 5 AMERICANS
(22%), SURPASSING
THE PERCENTAGE OF
THOSE WHO ARE BIBLE
ENGAGED (17%)

51% OF U.S. ADULTS
SAY POLITICS WOULD
BE MORE CIVIL IF
POLITICIANS ENGAGED
IN REGULAR BIBLE
READING

53% SAY
POLITICIANS WOULD
BE MORE EFFECTIVE
IF THEY READ THE
BIBLE MORE OFTEN

1 WHAT AMERICANS BELIEVE ABOUT THE BIBLE

A Holy Book

Americans overwhelmingly name the Bible as the book that comes to mind when they think of sacred literature or holy books (81%). This is particularly true among older generations and ethnic minorities—nine out of 10 older adults and black Americans cite the Bible as a holy book. Younger generations, however—especially Millennials (ages 18 to 31)—are less likely to point to the Bible as a holy book. And, as you would probably expect, those with no faith (including atheists, agnostics and "nones," who claim no religious affiliation) are less likely than the general population to choose the Bible. In fact, most of them say that no books are sacred (54%).*

The proportion of Americans who chooses the Bible is eight times that of the next most-frequently mentioned holy book, which is the Koran (10%). Other books considered sacred or holy—the Torah (5%) and the Book of Mormon (4%)—are mentioned by relatively few.

Americans who identify with faiths other than Christianity are more likely to mention the Koran (28%) and the Torah (15%), and less likely than average to name the Bible (45%). Twelve percent of U.S. adults do not consider any of these books to be holy, but the percentage is higher among Millennials (18%) and Gen-Xers (13%) than among their older counterparts, the Boomers (8%) and Elders (7%).

Regionally, residents of the Northeast (16%) and West (17%) are also more likely to prefer "none" than those in the Midwest (12%) or South (10%)—in keeping with the higher percentages of atheists, agnostics and the unaffiliated in those regions.

*Definitions for all of Barna's categories can be found in the Glossary.

WHEN THEY THINK OF SACRED LITERATURE, THE BIBLE COMES TO MIND FOR 8 OUT OF 10 U.S. ADULTS

AMERICANS WHO CONSIDER THE BIBLE A HOLY BOOK
% among U.S. adults 18 and older

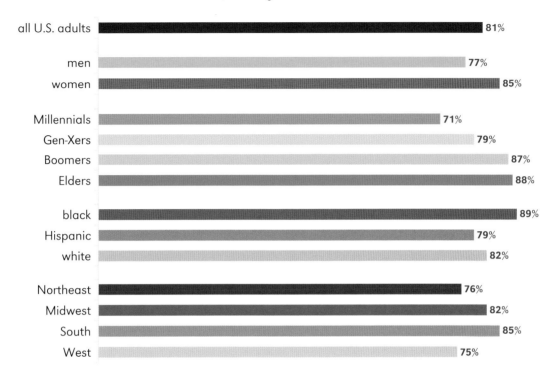

all U.S. adults	81%
men	77%
women	85%
Millennials	71%
Gen-Xers	79%
Boomers	87%
Elders	88%
black	89%
Hispanic	79%
white	82%
Northeast	76%
Midwest	82%
South	85%
West	75%

All this is in line with overall national trend of rising skepticism with regard to the Bible in particular and religion more generally. If these trend lines hold steady, there will be continuing downward pressure on the number of people (especially young people) who see the Bible as sacred.

A Guide to Meaningful Living

More than just a "holy book," a majority of people also sees the Bible as eminently practical for life. Two-thirds of U.S. adults agree with the statement, "The Bible contains everything a person needs to know to live a meaningful life" (48% strongly; 20% somewhat). Women (74%) are more convinced than men (64%) about the Bible's reliability in this regard, while black adults,

AMERICANS WHO CONSIDER THE BIBLE A COMPREHENSIVE GUIDE TO A MEANINGFUL LIFE

% strongly + somewhat agree among U.S. adults 18 and older

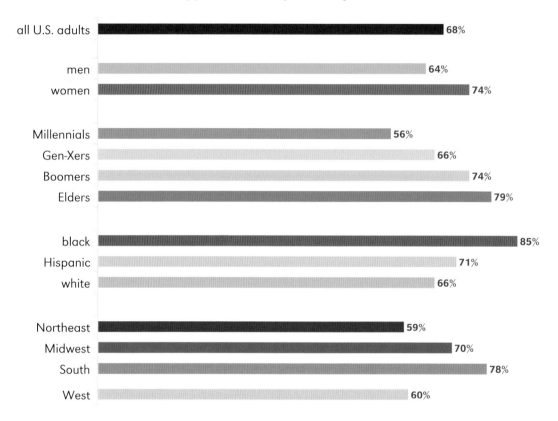

all U.S. adults	68%
men	64%
women	74%
Millennials	56%
Gen-Xers	66%
Boomers	74%
Elders	79%
black	85%
Hispanic	71%
white	66%
Northeast	59%
Midwest	70%
South	78%
West	60%

Americans over 50 and residents of the South also trust the Bible's guidance more than other population segments.

It's interesting to contrast this finding with the overwhelming cultural adoption of the "new moral code" examined in the Introduction. The tenets of the morality of self-fulfillment—pursue what you desire most in order to be fulfilled; the highest goal of life is to enjoy it—are not recommended by the Bible as guiding principles for life. In fact, three of the Gospels record Jesus saying, "If you want to save your own life, you will lose it; but if you lose your life for me and for the gospel, you will save it" (Mark 8:35, cf. Matt. 16:25; Luke 9:24). And yet many Americans seem to experience little cognitive dissonance between their acceptance of the new moral code and their view of the Bible as a guide for life.

Not surprisingly, few adherents to a religion other than Christianity (38%) and those of no faith (14%) agree that the Bible contains everything you need to know to live a meaningful life. Less predictably, however, nearly half (47%) of the "unchurched"—people who have not attended a worship service within the past six months—agree with the statement. This finding fits with other Barna data that shows the majority of unchurched Americans are actually "dechurched," meaning they were church attenders in the past but are no longer connected to a faith community. Most of these former churchgoers retain the contours of Christian belief, even if they are no longer practicing the faith.[3] This may represent another "window of opportunity" for church leaders, since many of the dechurched are still interested in and open to finding out how the Bible is meaningful for their lives.

An Influence on Society

With so many Americans believing the Bible is an effective guide for life, it's not surprising that a majority also believes U.S. society would be better off if the Bible were a greater influence (51%). Just over one-quarter, however, says the Scriptures' current level of cultural influence is just about right (28%), while 16 percent feel as if the Bible already has too much influence. Women, older adults and practicing Christians, in particular, would like to see a greater cultural role for the Bible, while men, younger Americans and those of no faith are somewhat less enthusiastic about increasing the Bible's influence on society. In fact, the most recent annual "State of the Bible" study found Millennials in 2016 slightly more likely to say the Bible has too much influence (34%) than that it has too little (30%).

ACCORDING TO A MAJORITY OF AMERICANS, U.S. SOCIETY WOULD BE BETTER OFF IF THE BIBLE WERE A GREATER INFLUENCE

THE BIBLE'S INFLUENCE ON U.S. SOCIETY
% among U.S. adults 18 and older

● too little   ● just right   ● too much   ● don't know

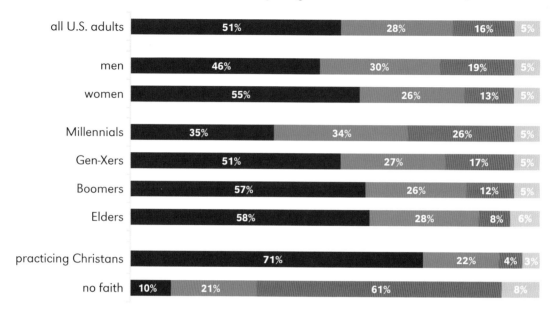

	too little	just right	too much	don't know
all U.S. adults	51%	28%	16%	5%
men	46%	30%	19%	5%
women	55%	26%	13%	5%
Millennials	35%	34%	26%	5%
Gen-Xers	51%	27%	17%	5%
Boomers	57%	26%	12%	5%
Elders	58%	28%	8%	6%
practicing Christans	71%	22%	4%	3%
no faith	10%	21%	61%	8%

2 BIBLE ENGAGEMENT IN AMERICA

When Barna and the American Bible Society launched the first "State of the Bible" study in 2011, one of the researchers' goals was to create a typology that could be used to track Americans' level of engagement with the Scriptures—involving both their views of the Bible's authority and their habit of Bible reading. The following graphic breaks down the four categories of Bible engagement. (These categories are used throughout this report. Here we look at the broad landscape of U.S. engagement; in later sections we'll examine key segments, such as practicing Christians and African Americans, whose Bible engagement differs markedly from the U.S. norm.)

FOUR TYPES OF BIBLE ENGAGEMENT

Barna designed a metric for Bible engagement based on *beliefs* about the Bible and *how often* people read it.

Bible Engaged

A person who is "engaged" has a high view of Scripture and reads the Bible four or more times per week.

Bible Friendly

The "friendly" person has a high view of Scripture, but reads it less frequently.

Bible Neutral

Someone who is "neutral" has a lower, but not negative, view of Scripture.

Bible Skeptic

Someone who is a "skeptic" believes the Bible is just another book of teachings written by men.

*For complete definitions, please visit the Glossary.

ENGAGEMENT ACROSS THE NATION: 2016

More than half of the U.S. population is *engaged* with or *friendly* toward the Bible. But about one in five adults is skeptical.

ALL U.S. ADULTS

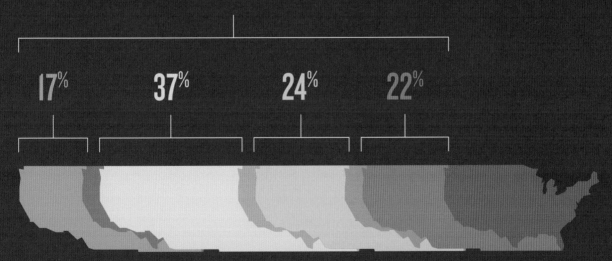

17%   37%   24%   22%

Barna / American Bible Society 2011–2016, N=12,062. Totals may not equal 100 percent due to rounding.

Bible engaged and *Bible friendly* people both have "high" views of the Scriptures, but those who are engaged read or listen to the Bible more frequently than those who are friendly. *Bible neutral* folks are less convinced about the Bible's supernatural origins, but are likewise unconvinced that it is merely the product of human hands. *Bible skeptics*, on the other hand, believe the Bible is just a book of teachings written by men, rather than the word of God.

The Word of God

To measure Bible engagement, researchers at Barna present survey respondents with a series of statements, asking them to choose one phrase (out of five options) that best describes their belief about the Bible. The best definition of the Bible, according to most Americans, is either the actual word of God (24%) or the inspired word of God with no errors (30%) or with some errors (14%).

In other words, a remarkable two-thirds of U.S. adults (68%) fall within the scope of historic Christian orthodoxy when it comes to their beliefs (one of the top three definitions), and just over half (54%) hold what is commonly known as a "high" view of the Scriptures (one of the top two definitions).

AMERICANS' BELIEFS ABOUT THE BIBLE

% among U.S. adults 18 and older

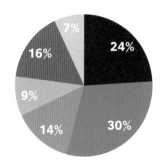

a. **The actual word of God** and should be taken literally, word for word

b. **The inspired word of God** and has no errors, although some verses are meant to be symbolic rather than literal

c. **The inspired word of God** but has some factual or historical errors

d. **Not inspired by God** but tells how the writers of the Bible understood the ways and principles of God

e. **Just another book of teaching written by men** that contains stories and advice

f. Other / don't know

BELIEFS ABOUT THE BIBLE

% among U.S. adults 18 and older

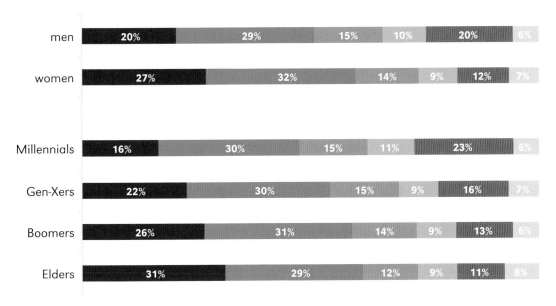

men	20%	29%	15%	10%	20%	6%
women	27%	32%	14%	9%	12%	7%
Millennials	16%	30%	15%	11%	23%	6%
Gen-Xers	22%	30%	15%	9%	16%	7%
Boomers	26%	31%	14%	9%	13%	6%
Elders	31%	29%	12%	9%	11%	8%

Some Americans are more convinced than others, however. For example, 31 percent of Elders 70 years and older subscribe to "the actual word of God" as the best definition of the Bible—making them twice as likely as Millennials to do so. Similarly, residents of the South (30%) are nearly twice as likely as Northeasterners (17%) to believe the Bible is the literal word of God.

A plurality of adherents to others faiths (34%) and a strong majority of those of no faith (66%) define the Bible as "just another book of teaching written by men that contains stories and advice." That definition is also preferred by a plurality of unchurched adults (31%) and by significant minorities of Northeasterners (21%) and Westerners (21%).

A Good Read

A majority of Americans may hold a "high" view of the Scriptures, but that doesn't mean a majority reads it—at least, not very often.

HOW FREQUENTLY AMERICANS READ THE BIBLE

% among U.S. adults 18 and older

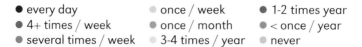

● every day   ○ once / week   ● 1-2 times year
● 4+ times / week   ● once / month   ● < once / year
● several times / week   ○ 3-4 times / year   ○ never

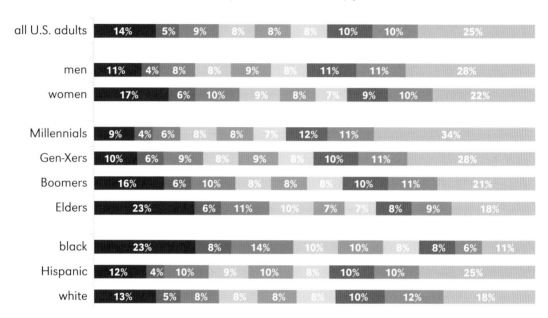

	every day	4+ times / week	several times / week	once / week	once / month	3-4 times / year	1-2 times year	< once / year	never
all U.S. adults	14%	5%	9%	8%	8%	8%	10%	10%	25%
men	11%	4%	8%	8%	9%	8%	11%	11%	28%
women	17%	6%	10%	9%	8%	7%	9%	10%	22%
Millennials	9%	4%	6%	8%	8%	7%	12%	11%	34%
Gen-Xers	10%	6%	9%	8%	9%	8%	10%	11%	28%
Boomers	16%	6%	10%	8%	8%	8%	10%	11%	21%
Elders	23%	6%	11%	10%	7%	7%	8%	9%	18%
black	23%	8%	14%	10%	10%	8%	8%	6%	11%
Hispanic	12%	4%	10%	9%	10%	8%	10%	10%	25%
white	13%	5%	8%	8%	8%	8%	10%	12%	18%

WOMEN, BLACK ADULTS AND OLDER AMERICANS SET THE PACE WHEN IT COMES TO BIBLE READING

Slightly more than one-third reads the Bible once a week or more frequently (36%) and the same proportion reads the Bible less than once a year or never (35%). The remaining three in 10 read somewhere between once a month and once a year.

As with perceptions of the Bible, women, black adults and older Americans are leaders when it comes to Bible reading.

Readership among U.S. adults may be lower than one might hope, but a healthy majority expresses a desire to read the Bible more (62%), and nearly one-quarter says they actually *did* increase their reading over the last year (23%). Even if some of these individuals are presenting an optimistic assessment of their Bible reading, we can see that the Bible benefits from a "halo effect"—that is, a majority of Americans are still "pro-Bible." This is an important indicator of opportunity for Christian leaders.

Bible Engagement in America

Different age, ethnic and faith cohorts have varying tendencies when it comes to Bible perceptions and reading habits, so these groups also tend to have higher or lower levels of Bible engagement based on those views and habits. For example, Elders and Boomers are generally more highly engaged than Millennials and Gen-Xers, and black adults are more engaged than Hispanics and whites. (We will explore these differences more deeply in Parts II and IV.)

62% OF AMERICANS WANT TO READ THE BIBLE MORE

BIBLE ENGAGEMENT IN AMERICA
% among U.S. adults 18 and older

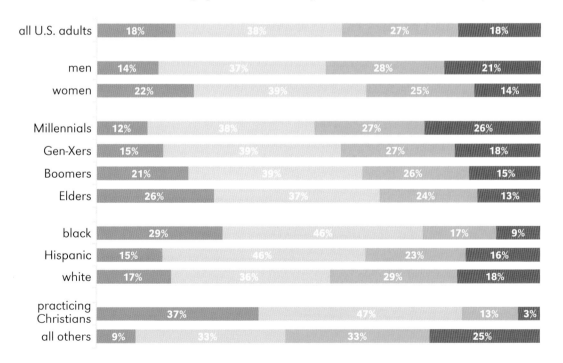

● Bible engaged ● Bible friendly ● Bible neutral ● Bible skeptic

	Bible engaged	Bible friendly	Bible neutral	Bible skeptic
all U.S. adults	18%	38%	27%	18%
men	14%	37%	28%	21%
women	22%	39%	25%	14%
Millennials	12%	36%	27%	26%
Gen-Xers	15%	39%	27%	18%
Boomers	21%	39%	26%	15%
Elders	26%	37%	24%	13%
black	29%	46%	17%	9%
Hispanic	15%	46%	23%	16%
white	17%	36%	29%	18%
practicing Christians	37%	47%	13%	3%
all others	9%	33%	33%	25%

The Bible & Discipleship

Barna partnered with The Navigators in a multiphase study to assess the state of discipleship in America's churches. Researchers interviewed senior pastors and discipleship leaders from across the country, as well as self-identified Christians from the general population, to identify what's working to help people grow spiritually. Since the Bible emerged in those interviews as a key factor in effective discipleship, the findings are included here as another "puzzle piece" in Barna's efforts to assemble a clear picture of the Bible in America.

Among church leaders—as one might expect—engagement with the Bible is considered a fundamental dimension of discipleship. Two-thirds of senior pastors (64%) and discipleship leaders (67%) say intentional, systematized study of the Bible is an essential element of spiritual formation. Six out of 10 senior pastors (60%) and three-quarters of discipleship leaders (73%) consider in-depth education about the Bible essential to spiritual growth. When it comes to practices that have the greatest impact on developing disciples, church leaders put personal Bible study (92%) and small group Bible study (88%) at the top of the list. Eight out of 10 say Bible teaching in weekly services makes an impact (81%), and two-thirds believe memorizing scripture is effective (65%).

Both practicing Christians and non-practicing Christians consider group Bible study to be a crucial practice in their spiritual development—yet key differences emerge in how much these two groups engage. Practicing Christians are also more likely to

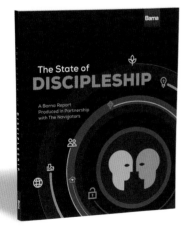

The State of Discipleship (Barna, 2015) is a Barna report produced in partnership with The Navigators.

say relationships formed through a small group Bible study have been an important aspect of their spiritual journey (61% vs. 22% of non-practicing Christians).

Among Christians who say spiritual growth is important to them, one-third of practicing Christians are currently in a small group Bible study (33%), yet only 6 percent of non-practicing Christians are in such a group, even though many of these same adults attest to the impact of a group study on their own spiritual life. The chart below shows the ways in which practicing Christians outpace others in their pursuit of scripture-oriented discipleship.

PARTICIPATION IN DISCIPLESHIP ACTIVITIES

% among Christians who say spiritual growth is very or somewhat important

● non-practicing Christian   ● practicing Christian

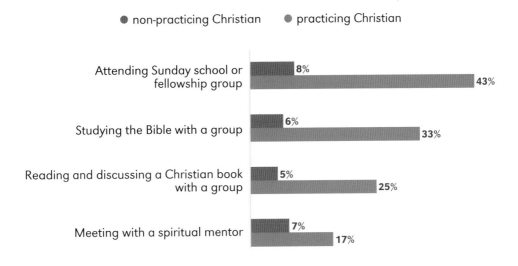

Attending Sunday school or fellowship group — 8% / 43%

Studying the Bible with a group — 6% / 33%

Reading and discussing a Christian book with a group — 5% / 25%

Meeting with a spiritual mentor — 7% / 17%

3 THE BIBLE IN ENTERTAINMENT

In recent years, the entertainment sector seems to have turned back to one of its favorite sources: the Bible. In past decades, films like *The Ten Commandments, Ben-Hur, The Passion of the Christ* and *The Prince of Egypt* have been critical and box office successes. The latest crop of faith-inspired titles includes films like *Noah, Exodus, Son of God, God's Not Dead, Risen, The Young Messiah, The Bible* miniseries, a new remake of *Ben-Hur, Miracles from Heaven* and *Last Days in the Desert.* Barna continues to explore how viewing religious content onscreen affects the way people view Christianity in everyday life. There are a number of insights that are relevant to *The Bible in America.*

First, it's not surprising that practicing Christians are the group most likely to be aware of and interested in viewing films or shows with Christian content. The three in 10 Americans who are most likely to prioritize and practice their faith represent more than 70 million adults nationwide. Generally, practicing Christians are most receptive to entertainment that contains clear messaging and implications for their faith. In other words, when content is made *for* practicing Christians, they generally respond most favorably toward it.

Second, the market for faith-driven content is not exclusive to practicing Christians. The U.S. population continues to be quite open to such entertainment, as long as it's *entertaining.* Interestingly, Bible-driven movies like *Noah* and *Exodus* drew audiences in roughly equal proportions across all faith segments. Another example: Among all adults, 14 percent said they had watched some portion of the *The Bible* miniseries on the History Channel in 2014. While one-quarter of practicing Christians said they tuned in, this televised program also generated reported viewership among 10 percent of non-practicing Christians (who represent an audience

PRACTICING CHRISTIANS ARE MOST RECEPTIVE TO ENTERTAINMENT THAT CONTAINS CLEAR MESSAGING AND IMPLICATIONS FOR THEIR FAITH

THE BIBLE ON SCREEN

Which of the following have you seen?

	% ALL ADULTS	% PRACTICING CHRISTIANS	% NON-PRACTICING CHRISTIANS	% OTHER FAITH	% NO FAITH
The Bible miniseries on the History Channel *	14	25	10	18	13
Noah	11	10	12	9	12
Exodus: Gods and Kings	7	6	7	5	5

* % who "definitely" recall tuning into some portion of the miniseries

of 100 million adults!), 8 percent of adherents to faiths other than Christianity and 3 percent of the non-religious audience.

Third, we find evidence that faith-driven entertainment can change perceptions and activity. Can Bible entertainment encourage Bible engagement? It seems likely. For example, among adults who increased their Bible readership in 2013, one in nine (11%) said watching *The Bible* miniseries inspired them to read the Scriptures more. This may seem like a small overall percentage, but it represents a huge number of people in an aggregate sense.

Also, some faith-oriented films seem to impact how some people think about Christianity. When asked if any movies from the last two years made them think more seriously about religion, spirituality or religious faith, 13 percent of U.S. adults say they have been influenced by film in this manner. The most commonly mentioned movies included *God's Not Dead, The Bible* miniseries, *Noah, Courageous* and *Heaven is for Real*.

Finally, people have mixed views on how well Hollywood portrays Christianity. Just over one-quarter of all adults (28%) feels Hollywood's general representation of Christianity is sometimes positive, sometimes negative; another 21 percent say it is neutral, neither positive nor negative. Practicing Christians hold a wide range of feelings about Hollywood's treatment of Christianity. The most common perceptions are that Hollywood portrays their faith negatively (25%) or depicts it with mixed results, sometimes positively and sometimes negatively (27%). Only one in nine practicing Christians (11%) believes that Hollywood describes Christianity positively.

In a crowded marketplace, the commercial success of Bible-oriented and faith-driven fare is all but certain. There's a good chance studios will continue producing content inspired by the Christian faith since there is a built-in audience of adults who identify as Christian and many of the stories are well-known to most Americans.

DOES HOLLYWOOD "GET" CHRISTIANITY?

What is your opinion of Hollywood's treatment of Christianity?

	% ALL ADULTS	% PRACTICING CHRISTIANS	% NON-PRACTICING CHRISTIANS	% OTHER FAITH	% NO FAITH
They generally portray it positively	9	11	9	10	11
They generally portray it negatively	14	25	9	13	3
Neutral: neither positively or negatively	21	17	23	16	23
Mixed: sometimes negatively, sometimes positively	28	27	28	18	20
They rely heavily on stereotypes	8	9	7	7	8
don't know	20	9	25	36	35

Percentages may not equal 100% due to rounding

4 THE BIBLE IN SOCIETY & POLITICS

One of the key findings of *The Bible in America* is the degree to which the Bible is central to Americans' views of a good society. When people are asked to choose from a list of literary works the one book they believe has had the greatest impact on humanity, the Bible tops the list—even among the more Bible-resistant Millennials.

Yet there seems to be growing discomfort, as noted earlier, with how much influence the Bible wields today in U.S. society. The tracking numbers show rising levels of skepticism about the Bible's role in culture. This is due in large measure to the

THE BIBLE'S IMPACT

Which of the following do you think has had the most impact on humanity?

	% ALL ADULTS	% MILLENNIALS 18–31	% GEN-XERS 32–50	% BOOMERS 51–69	% ELDERS 70+
the Bible	64	51	64	69	76
On the Origin of Species	6	8	6	5	4
the Koran	6	6	7	5	4
The Republic by Plato	5	9	5	5	1
The Art of War by Sun Tzu	4	9	2	2	1
none of these	6	7	7	6	4
not sure	10	10	9	10	11

PERCEIVED IMPACT ON SOCIETY

Do you think the Bible has too much, too little or just the right amount of influence in U.S. society?	2011	2012	2013	2014	2015	2016
too little influence	54	47	56	50	51	46
just right	28	29	26	30	27	30
too much influence	13	16	13	16	19	19
not sure	5	7	6	6	3	5

increasingly mixed feelings of Millennials, who are twice as likely as Boomers (26% vs. 12%) and three times more likely than Elders (8%) to say the Bible has too much cultural influence.

Given the skepticism among younger adults about the role of the Bible in culture, it's not surprising to find there is also ambivalence about the Scriptures' impact on politics and governance. An overall majority of U.S. adults say politics would be more civil (51%) and those who govern would be more effective (53%) if politicians read the Bible on a regular basis—but those majorities are not spread evenly across the population.

Young adults are less convinced than older Americans that regular Bible reading is the solution to uncivil and ineffective politics. Only about one-third of Millennials and half of Gen-Xers say politics would be more civil (31% Millennials, 47% Gen-Xers) and politicians would be more effective (34% Millennials, 49% Gen-Xers) if they read the Bible more often. By comparison, two-thirds of Boomers and three-quarters of Elders believe politics would be more civil and effective with regular Bible reading.

THE EFFECT OF REGULAR BIBLE READING ON POLITICANS

% "yes" among U.S. adults 18 and older

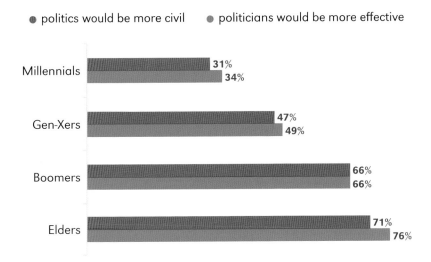

● politics would be more civil   ● politicians would be more effective

Millennials — 31% / 34%

Gen-Xers — 47% / 49%

Boomers — 66% / 66%

Elders — 71% / 76%

These numbers—and the differences between generations—signal a sea change in U.S. society. The two older generations of Americans (Boomers and Elders) are consistent in their belief that Bible engagement would make society a better place, yet Gen-Xers and especially Millennials are quite resistant to that notion. Even in the midst of a lot of generational differences, these represent some of the most significant gaps on any subject in this report. Younger generations are reprioritizing the Bible's role in public life.

In an analysis of a group we call "Bible minded"—who believe the Bible is accurate in all the principles it teaches and have read the Bible within the past week—compared with the general U.S. population, Barna found that the Bible minded are comparatively cause- and issues-oriented when it comes to political concerns. Rating how much influence each issue has on their voting habits, Bible-minded people are more likely to prioritize religious liberty (66% vs. 34% among all adults), abortion (46% vs. 32%), marriage (55% vs. 33%) and poverty (51% vs. 42%).

YOUNGER GENERATIONS ARE REPRIORITIZING THE BIBLE'S ROLE IN PUBLIC LIFE

Interestingly, Bible-minded adults tend to be skeptical about the government's ability to change for the better and disappointed when change doesn't happen. At the same time, Bible-minded adults are more likely than average to self-describe as politically active, to be personally invested in the political process, and to be hopeful they can make a difference by being politically involved.

PERCEPTIONS OF POLITICS
% agree strongly among U.S. adults 18 and older

● all U.S. adults ● Bible-minded adults

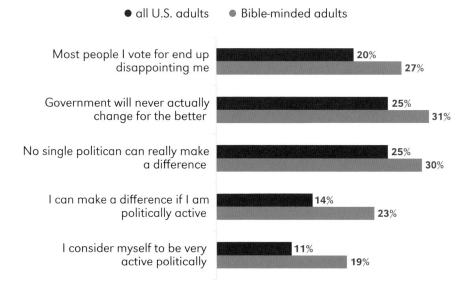

Most people I vote for end up disappointing me — 20% / 27%

Government will never actually change for the better — 25% / 31%

No single politican can really make a difference — 25% / 30%

I can make a difference if I am politically active — 14% / 23%

I consider myself to be very active politically — 11% / 19%

5 BIBLE-MINDED CITIES

Each year, the American Bible Society and Barna look at how each major metro area in the U.S. views the Bible. The annual "Bible-Minded Cities Report," based on interviews with 65,064 adults over a 10-year period, shows how people living in the nation's 100 largest media markets view and use the Bible. Individuals who report reading the Bible in a typical week and who strongly assert the

Bible is accurate in all the principles it teaches are considered "Bible-minded." This definition captures *action* and *attitude*—those who both engage and esteem the Christian Scriptures. Thus, the rankings reflect an overall openness or resistance to the Bible in various U.S. cities. With a host of religiously charged social issues sparking national conversations, it's important for Christian pastors and leaders to note how the Bible stacks up in their communities.

As in previous years, the South remains the most Bible-minded region of the country in 2016, with *all* of the top 10 cities located below the Mason-Dixon line. After dropping down to the runner-up position last year from the top spot three years in a row, Chattanooga, Tennessee, reclaims its title as the most Bible-minded city in America. Fifty-two percent of its population qualifies as Bible-minded. Birmingham / Anniston / Tuscaloosa, Alabama—the most Bible-minded city of 2015—dropped to second place (51%).

Third, fourth and fifth places went to Roanoke / Lynchburg, Virginia (48%), Shreveport, Louisiana (47%) and Tri-Cities, Tennessee (47%), respectively. Other cities in the top 10 include Charlotte, North Carolina (46%), Little Rock / Pine Bluff, Arkansas (46%), Knoxville, Tennessee (45%), the Greenville, South Carolina, and Asheville, North Carolina, area (44%) and Lexington, Kentucky (44%).

The bottom five cities are primarily in the Northeast or on the East Coast, with the exception of one in the Midwest. The least Bible-minded city in 2016—Albany / Schenectady / Troy, New York—moved up one spot from last year, with only 10 percent of residents qualifying as Bible-minded. Boston, Massachusetts (11%) moved from third to second place while Providence, Rhode Island (12%)—the least Bible-minded city in 2015—dropped two spots to third place. The only Midwestern city to make the top five was Cedar Rapids, Iowa (13%), followed by Buffalo, New York (13%), to round out the list.

Other cities in the bottom 10 include Las Vegas, Nevada (14%), the San Francisco, California, area (15%), Hartford / New Haven, Connecticut (16%), Phoenix / Prescott, Arizona (16%), and Salt Lake City, Utah (17%).

AMERICA'S BIBLE-MINDED CITIES 2016

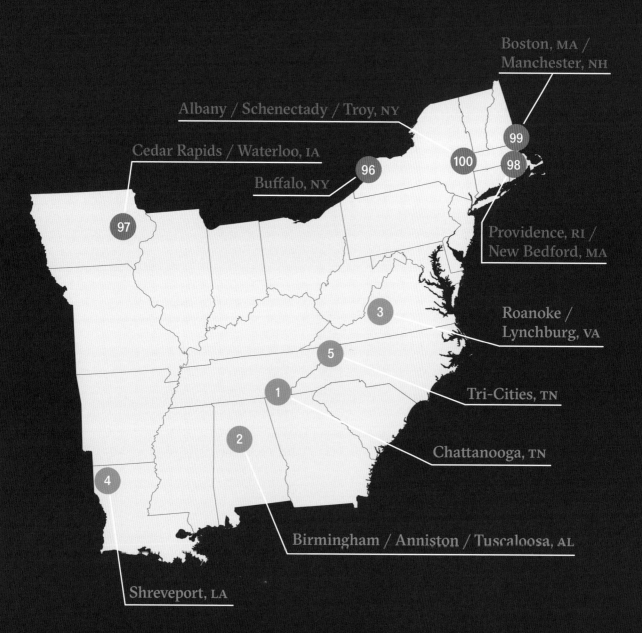

Boston, MA / Manchester, NH

Albany / Schenectady / Troy, NY

Cedar Rapids / Waterloo, IA

Buffalo, NY

99

100

98

96

97

Providence, RI / New Bedford, MA

3

Roanoke / Lynchburg, VA

5

1

Tri-Cities, TN

2

Chattanooga, TN

4

Birmingham / Anniston / Tuscaloosa, AL

Shreveport, LA

WHAT IS A BIBLE-MINDED CITY?

Respondents who report reading the Bible within the past seven days and who agree strongly in the accuracy of the Bible are classified as "Bible minded."

#	City	POP %	#	City	POP %	#	City	POP %
1	Chattanooga, TN	52	33	Indianapolis, IN	32	64	Milwaukee, WI	23
2	Birmingham / Anniston / Tuscaloosa, AL	51	34	Kansas City, KS-MO	32	65	Toledo, OH	23
3	Roanoke / Lynchburg, VA	48	35	Cincinnati, OH	32	66	Detroit, MI	22
4	Shreveport, LA	47	36	San Antonio, TX	32	67	Minneapolis / St. Paul, MN	22
5	Tri-Cities, TN	47	37	New Orleans, LA	32	68	Pittsburgh, PA	22
6	Charlotte, NC	46	38	Richmond / Petersburg, VA	32	69	Baltimore, MD	22
7	Little Rock / Pine Bluff, AR	45	39	Tulsa, OK	32	70	San Diego, CA	22
8	Knoxville, TN	45	40	Dayton, OH	32	71	Fresno / Visalia, CA	22
9	Greenville / Spartanburg / Anderson, SC / Ashville, NC	44	41	Charleston, SC	32	72	Des Moines / Ames, IA	22
10	Lexington, KY	44	42	Norfolk / Portsmouth / Newport News, VA	31	73	Omaha, NE	22
11	Springfield, MO	44	43	South Bend / Elkhart, IN	31	74	Syracuse, NY	22
12	Huntsville-Decatur-Florence, AL	42	44	Davenport, IA / Rock Island / Moline, IL	31	75	Seattle / Tacoma, WA	21
13	Savannah, GA	42	45	Fort Smith / Fayetteville / Springdale-Rogers, AR	31	76	Cleveland / Akron / Canton, OH	21
14	Oklahoma City, OK	41	46	St. Louis, MO	28	77	Flint / Saginaw / Bay City, MI	21
15	Jackson, MS	41	47	Austin, TX	27	78	Chicago, IL	20
16	Nashville, TN	39	48	Albuquerque / Santa Fe, NM	27	79	Sacramento / Stockton / Modesto, CA	20
17	Louisville, KY	39	49	Harlingen / Weslaco / McAllen / Brownsville, TX	27	80	Los Angeles, CA	19
18	Wichita / Hutchinson, KS	39	50	El Paso, TX / Las Cruces, NM	27	81	Denver, CO	19
19	Baton Rouge, LA	38	51	Houston, TX	26	82	Wilkes-Barre / Scranton, PA	19
20	Grand Rapids / Kalamazoo / Battle Creek, MI	37	52	Spokane, WA	26	83	Ft. Myers / Naples, FL	19
21	Greensboro / High Point / Winston-Salem, NC	37	53	Portland, OR	25	84	Tucson / Sierra Vista, AZ	19
22	Charleston / Huntington, WV	37	54	Columbus, OH	25	85	Rochester, NY	19
23	Columbia, SC	37	55	Champaign / Springfield / Decatur, IL	25	86	Portland / Auburn, ME	19
24	Raleigh / Durham / Fayetteville, NC	36	56	Colorado Springs / Pueblo, CO	25	87	Washington, DC / Hagerstown, MD	18
25	Memphis, TN	36	57	Philadelphia, PA	24	88	Madison, WI	18
26	Greenville / New Bern / Washington, NC	36	58	Miami / Ft. Lauderdale, FL	24	89	Burlington / Plattsburgh, VT	18
27	Paducah, KY / Cape Girardeau, MO / Harrisburg, IL / Mt. Vernon, IL	36	59	Green Bay / Appleton, WI	24	90	New York, NY	17
28	Dallas / Fort Worth, TX	35	60	West Palm Beach / Fort Pierce, FL	23	91	Salt Lake City, UT	17
29	Jacksonville, FL	34	61	Tampa / St. Petersburg / Sarasota, FL	23	92	Phoenix / Prescott, AZ	16
30	Mobile, AL / Pensacola / Fort Walton, FL	34	62	Harrisburg / Lancaster / Lebanon / York, PA	23	93	Hartford / New Haven, CT	16
31	Waco / Temple / Bryan, TX	34	63	Orlando / Daytona Beach / Melbourne, FL	23	94	San Francisco / Oakland / San Jose, CA	15
32	Atlanta, GA	33				95	Las Vegas, NV	14
						96	Buffalo, NY	13
						97	Cedar Rapids / Waterloo, IA	13
						98	Providence, RI / New Bedford, MA	12
						99	Boston, MA / Manchester, NH	11
						100	Albany / Schenectady / Troy, NY	10

The data reported in this table are based upon telephone and online interviews with nationwide random samples of 65,064 adults conducted over a 10-year period, ending in August 2015. The maximum margin of sampling error associated with the aggregate sample is ±0.4 percentage points at the 95% confidence level.

DR. JOHN FEA

John Fea, PhD, teaches American history at Messiah College in Mechanicsburg, Pennsylvania. He is the author of several books, most recently, *The Bible Cause: A History of the American Bible Society* (Oxford University Press, 2016).

The State of the Bible 1816

On October 28, 1996, an article in the business section of the *New York* Times reported that the $200 million market for Bibles "is flat as a leather Bible cover."[4] A director for marketing at Oxford University Press suggested that the American market for the holy book had reached a saturation point. Most experts blamed the glut in the market on the rise of the so-called big box stores—Barnes & Noble, Walmart and Sam's Club—that also sold Bibles. According to the *Times* article, the latest American Bible Society translation to hit the market, the Contemporary English Version, had only captured 1 percent of the Bible market for its publisher, Thomas Nelson.

One reader who was disturbed by the *Times* article was Eugene Habecker, then-president and CEO of American Bible Society. Habecker penned a letter to the editor that was published a few days later. He did not dispute the fact that Bible sales were going through a sluggish season. What bothered Habecker the most about the article was the fact that so many Americans owned a Bible (he estimated that there was one in at least 90 percent of homes), but few had any idea what was in it or how to engage with its content. "The people who have Bibles . . . don't use them enough," Habecker wrote, "or when they do, they don't remember what they have read." Habecker concluded that American Bible Society, despite its impressive distribution numbers, was not doing enough to teach people how to use the Bible. The seeds for the current program of "Bible engagement" was born.

Elias Boudinot, the first President of American Bible Society, would have agreed with Habecker. But when he led the charge to found American Bible Society in 1816, he was much more concerned with *distribution* than with *use*. Boudinot believed there were a large number of people living in the United States who did not own a copy of the Christian Scriptures and who would benefit from having access to the Bible. He believed that the Bible was a tool for evangelism and, with the help of the Holy Spirit, any reader of the Bible could decipher its meaning and be transformed by its message. The goal was to simply put a copy of the Bible—without interpretive notes or comments—in the hands of as many people as possible and let God do the rest.

Like the organization in the 21st century, Boudinot and the founders of American Bible Society were concerned about the state of the Bible in the nation. Their concern was twofold. First, people needed a copy of the Bible. The American Bible Society founders received regular reports from Western missionaries who lamented the desperate need for Bibles on the frontier. One of those missionaries was Samuel J. Mills of the Massachusetts Missionary Society. In 1812 Mills joined fellow missionary John Schermerhorn on a year-long tour through the Southern and Western portions of the United States. Their mission was evangelistic, but they were also charged with gaining information—survey data, if you will—about the state of Bible ownership in these areas. Upon his return, Mills claimed that there were between 40,000 and 50,000 French Catholics in Louisiana who did not own Bibles. He estimated that in at least 13,000 Bibles were needed in St. Louis to provide one for every family. Thirty thousand more Bibles were needed for the same reason in Kentucky, Tennessee, Indiana, Illinois and Mississippi. Mills lamented that the "whole country," from "Lake Erie to the Gulf of Mexico," is "as the valley of the shadow of death" due to a lack of Bibles.

The founders' second concern was the role Bible should play in the development of the American republic. Boudinot believed

BOUDINOT BELIEVED THE BIBLE WAS A TOOL FOR EVANGELISM AND, WITH THE HELP OF THE HOLY SPIRIT, ANY READER COULD BE TRANSFOMRED BY ITS MESSAGE

AMERICAN BIBLE SOCIETY LED A REVOLUTION IN RELIGIOUS PRINTING AND PUBLICATION THAT BROUGHT THE BIBLE AND CHRISTIANITY TO ORDINARY PEOPLE IN 19TH-CENTURY AMERICA

that the United States, especially under the leadership of Thomas Jefferson and his followers, was moving in a secular direction. On several occasions he used his pen to defend orthodox Protestantism against threats from "infidels" seeking to undermine the role the Bible must play in American culture. For example, in 1801, fearful that heretics and unbelievers were infiltrating American society and influencing its youth, Boudinot published a book-length critique of Thomas Paine's *The Age of Reason*, which he perceived as an attack on traditional Christianity. Boudinot called his book *The Age of Revelation or The Age of Reason Shewn to be an Age of Infidelity*. In this book Boudinot defended traditional Christian doctrines such as the divine inspiration of the Bible, the Virgin conception and deity of Christ, and Christ's resurrection from the dead. It was clear that Boudinot and the founders of American Bible Society wanted a Christian republic that was rooted in the teachings of the Scriptures.

Over the course of three or four decades following the creation of the organization in 1816, Boudinot's prayers were answered. American Bible Society published and distributed millions of Bibles throughout the United States and the world. A massive evangelical revival swept the nation in those years, essentially Christianizing the culture and bringing moral reform to the republic. And American Bible Society led a revolution in religious printing and publication that brought the Bible and Christianity to ordinary people in 19th-century America.

When Eugene Habecker took American Bible Society down the path of Bible engagement in the 1990s, a path the organization follows to this day, he was continuing the work begun two centuries ago by men and women empowered by the same Spirit and enlivened by the same vision.

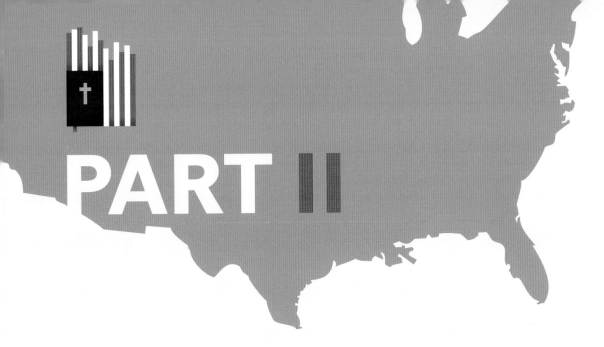

PART II

THE BIBLE IN A CHANGING CONTEXT

Twenty-five years ago, in 1991, 45 percent of U.S. adults told Barna they read the Bible at least once a week. In 2009, 46 percent reported doing so. These percentages were remarkably consistent over the course of nearly two decades. In the intervening years, however, Bible reading has become less widespread, especially among the youngest adults. As more and more Millennials join the adult population, the national average continues to decline.

Today, about one-third of all U.S. adults report reading the Bible once a week or more. The percentage is highest among Elders (49%) and lowest among Millennials (24%).

What else is changing? And what are the factors catalyzing the changes? Part II follows the "State of the Bible" data over six years to identify trends in Bible beliefs and practices. Asking a national representative sample of adults the same questions year after year allows researchers to track the country's shifting perceptions of the Scriptures—from rising skepticism to increased digital Bible reading.

A few trends to notice:

- Bible literacy is waning among younger generations of Americans—but not among practicing Christians.
- Millennials (and Gen-Xers, to some extent) are more indifferent to or skeptical toward the Bible. This goes for both beliefs and perceptions, and for ideas about its usefulness today.
- Young adults are adopting digital Bible tools more readily than older Americans, and some say these tools are increasing their engagement with the Scriptures.

GENERATION GAP

The Bible has been a part of American life since the first English colonists settled Jamestown in 1607. For nearly 400 years its well-known words, stories, people and principles informed public discourse and formed the national character and shared worldview. Younger generations, however, are loosening the Bible's grip on the American soul.

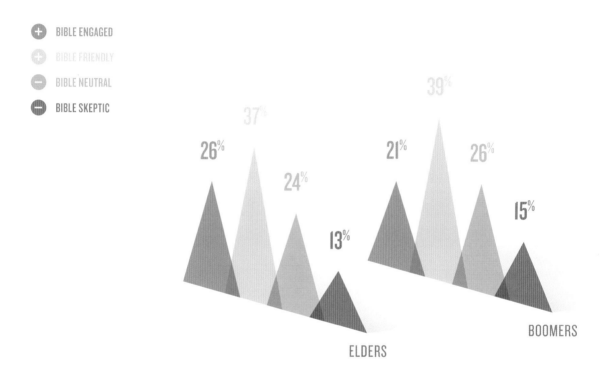

⊕ BIBLE ENGAGED
⊕ BIBLE FRIENDLY
⊖ BIBLE NEUTRAL
⊖ BIBLE SKEPTIC

ELDERS
26%   37%   24%   13%

BOOMERS
21%   39%   26%   15%

THE RISE OF BIBLE SKEPTICS

PERCENT OF ADULTS THAT QUALIFY AS BIBLE SKEPTICS

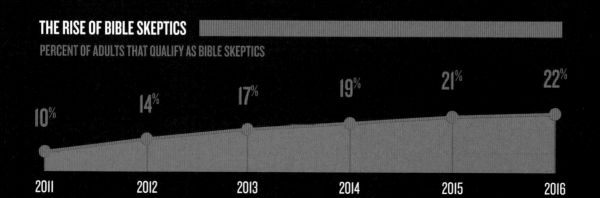

2011	2012	2013	2014	2015	2016
10%	14%	17%	19%	21%	22%

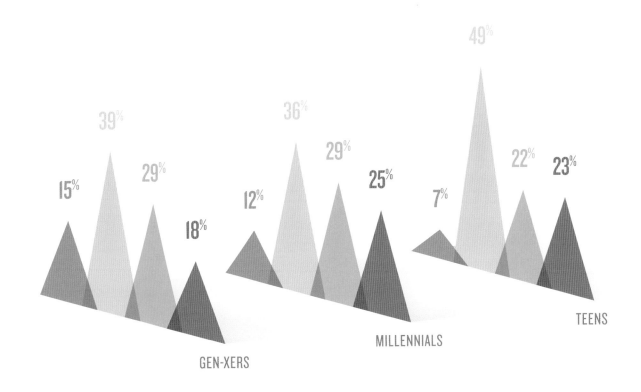

15% 39% 29% 18%

GEN-XERS

12% 36% 29% 25%

MILLENNIALS

7% 49% 22% 23%

TEENS

TOP REASONS PEOPLE GIVE FOR DECREASED BIBLE ENGAGEMENT

58%

TOO BUSY WITH LIFE'S
RESPONSIBILITIES

17%

BECAME ATHEIST OR
AGNOSTIC

17%

DECIDED TO LEAVE THE
CHURCH ALTOGETHER

12%

A DIFFICULT EXPERIENCE IN MY LIFE
CAUSED ME TO DOUBT MY FAITH

BIBLE OWNERSHIP

The percentage of Americans who say yes, they own a copy of the Bible, has held steady over the past half-decade. Nearly nine out of 10 adults say there is at least one Bible at home, and the median number of Bibles per household is 3.0.

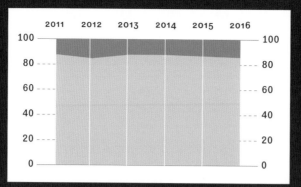

No

Yes

THE BIBLE THROUGH THE YEARS

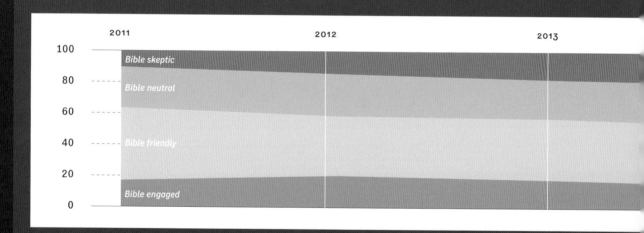

Bible skeptic

Bible neutral

Bible friendly

Bible engaged

WHAT IS THE BIBLE, EXACTLY?

Americans' views on how best to describe the Bible have remained fairly consistent over time—except among Millennials, which we'll explore in part IV. As more Millennials have emerged into adulthood since 2011, they have begun to tip the Bible-engagement scales toward greater skepticism.

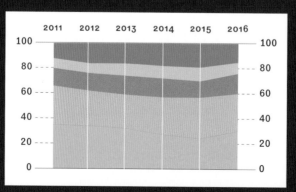

just another book of teachings written by men that contain stories and advice

not inspired, tells how writers understood the ways and principles of God

inspired word of God, has some factual or historical errors

inspired word of God, no errors, some verses symbolic

actual word of God and should be taken literally, word for word

HABITS OF BIBLE READING

Bible readership among U.S. adults has also been notably stable since 2011. About one-quarter never reads the Scriptures, while another one-quarter reads the Bible a few times a week or more. The other half of the population falls somewhere in between.

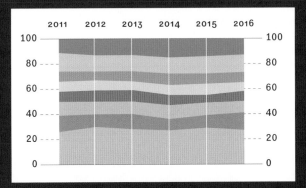

every day

several times/4+ times a week

once a week
once a month
three or four times a year
once or twice a year
less than once a year

never

Barna and American Bible Society have tracked Americans' views of and engagement with the Bible since 2011. Bible ownership and reading habits have remained fairly consistent through the years – but there is a clear downward trend when it comes to views on the Bible's trustworthiness and influence.

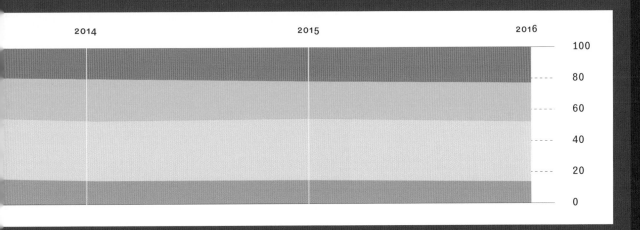

THE BIBLE'S INFLUENCE ON SOCIETY

Fewer people today than in 2011 say the Bible's influence on society is too limited—and the number of Americans who says it holds too much sway over society is increasing.

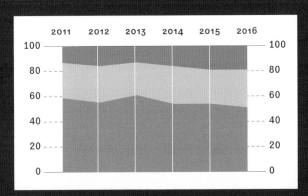

too much influence

just right

too little influence

Barna / American Bible Society 2011–2016, *N*=12,062. Totals may not equal 100 percent due to rounding.

THE BIBLE GOES DIGITAL

A good ol' fashioned print edition of the Bible remains the most common format among American Bible readers – but the popularity of digital versions, whether online or through a smartphone or tablet app, is growing . . . especially among younger generations.

PERCENT AMONG BIBLE READERS WHO REPORT USING
EACH FORMAT WITHIN THE PREVIOUS YEAR

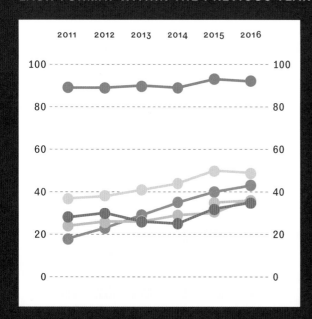

read from a print version of the Bible

used the Internet on a computer to read Bible content
listened to teaching about the Bible via podcast
searched for Bible verses or Bible content on a smartphone or cell phone
listened to an audio version of the Bible
downloaded or used a Bible app on a smartphone

PREFERENCES BY GENERATION

MILLENNIALS

print **90%**
web browser **75%**
smartphone search **78%**
smartphone or tablet app **62%**
podcast **39%**
audio version **34%**

GEN-XERS

print **91%**
web browser **53%**
smartphone search **47%**
smartphone or tablet app **47%**
podcast **38%**
audio version **37%**

BOOMERS

print **93%**
web browser **42%**
smartphone search **33%**
podcast **37%**
audio version **33%**
smartphone or tablet app **30%**

ELDERS

print **96%**
podcast **34%**
audio version **30%**
web browser **21%**
smartphone search **14%**
smartphone or tablet app **7%**

Barna / American Bible Society 2011–2016, N=12,062. Totals may not equal 100 percent due to rounding.

6 BIBLE LITERACY

One of the themes of *The Bible in America*, and more generally of Barna's recent work, is that Americans increasingly minimize external sources of authority, such as institutions and religious texts, as they determine how life ought to be lived. Within this changing context, how familiar are people with the Bible's background, people, stories and principles? In each year of American Bible Society's "The State of the Bible" research, Barna asks U.S. adults about the Bible's contents in order to gauge their biblical literacy.

Here is one example: Survey respondents were presented four statements and asked to identify the phrase that comes directly from the Bible.

- The truth will set you free.
- To thine own self be true.
- God helps those who help themselves.
- God works in mysterious ways.

Only 24 percent of adults were able to correctly identify "The truth will set you free" as a direct quote from the Bible. Instead, most others incorrectly selected the following phrases: "God works in mysterious ways" (36%); "To thine own self be true" (17%); and "God helps those who help themselves" (13%).

A combined majority of Americans believes the three latter statements are direct quotes from the Bible and, interestingly, the sentiment of these phrases points to the morality of self-fulfillment. As indicated in the Introduction, millions of adults (including many practicing Christians) believe the best way to find yourself is to look within yourself—so it is little wonder that self-oriented, feel-good phrases would wrongly be categorized as holy writ. Part of the Christian community's focus in the coming years must be a reorientation toward the Scriptures as a filter for our lives, rather than trusting ourselves as a filter for understanding

AMERICANS INCREASINGLY MINIMIZE EXTERNAL SOURCES OF AUTHORITY, SUCH AS INSTITUTIONS AND RELIGIOUS TEXTS, AS THEY DETERMINE HOW LIFE OUGHT TO BE LIVED

WE MUST REORIENT TOWARD THE SCRIPTURES AS A FILTER FOR OUR LIVES, RATHER THAN TRUSTING OURSELVES AS A FILTER FOR UNDERSTANDING THE SCRIPTURES

the Scriptures. This need is a wide-open window of opportunity for leaders concerned with helping people engage with the Bible.

Barna's study of biblical literacy also reveals that most Americans retain some level of familiarity with the Bible. This does not mean that they understand the implications of the Scriptures for their lives—or even that they are familiar with the document itself (for example, only one-quarter knows the New Testament was originally written in Greek).

When it comes to some of the basic elements, however, millions of Americans retain "muscle memory" of the Bible. A majority of Americans, for example, is able to correctly identify the first book in the Bible as Genesis. Most know that the "3" in John 3:16 refers to the chapter reference. More than half know the apostle Paul was also known as Saul, and most are also able to correctly identify the biblical book named after a woman (Esther). Just fewer than half are able to identify the names of the first five books of the Bible.

Furthermore, Americans remain confident that some of the most amazing stories in the Bible can be taken at face value. This is a slight twist on Bible literacy; it's not just whether people *know* the stories of the Bible, but whether they *believe* they actually happened. Survey respondents were asked if they thought a specific story in the Bible was "literally true, meaning it happened exactly as described in the Bible" or whether they thought the story was "meant to illustrate a principle but is not to be taken literally." Several well-known Bible stories were then offered for consideration.

Surprisingly, the most significant Bible story of all—"the story of Jesus Christ rising from the dead, after being crucified and buried"—is also the most widely embraced. Three out of four adults say they interpreted that narrative literally (75%), while only one out of five said they did not (19%). This is remarkable. Although millions who believe in the fact of the Resurrection may not understand how to connect the dots to their daily lives, the Bible's record of these events powerfully resonates with them even today. The window of believability is still open for millions of people.

The account of the prophet Daniel surviving in the lion's den is deemed literally true by two-thirds of adults (65%). Two out of three Americans believe that Moses literally parted the Red Sea to allow the Israelites to escape from the Egyptians (64%). The Bible says the young shepherd David killed a giant warrior, Goliath, with stones and a slingshot; nearly two-thirds of Americans accept that story as accurate (63%). These findings are evidence that belief in the supernatural and miracles endures, and that the Bible's culture-shaping influence remains strong in America.

Despite these favorable realities, Bible literacy is in decline among younger adults. They are less likely to have the "muscle memory" of Bible knowledge. As the chart shows, Millennials score lower

MOST AMERICANS RETAIN SOME LEVEL OF FAMILIARITY WITH THE BIBLE—BUT LITERACY IS IN DECLINE AMONG YOUNGER ADULTS

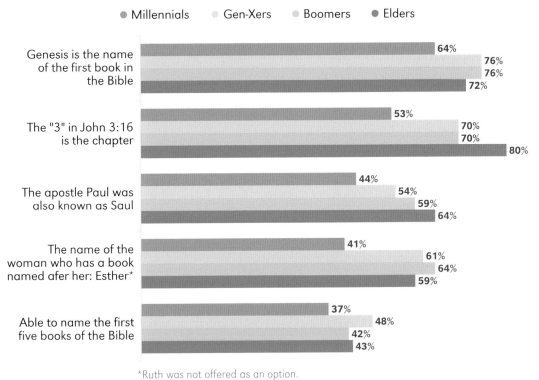

BIBLICAL LITERACY
% among U.S. adults 18 and older

● Millennials   ● Gen-Xers   ● Boomers   ● Elders

Genesis is the name of the first book in the Bible
- 64%
- 76%
- 76%
- 72%

The "3" in John 3:16 is the chapter
- 53%
- 70%
- 70%
- 80%

The apostle Paul was also known as Saul
- 44%
- 54%
- 59%
- 64%

The name of the woman who has a book named afer her: Esther*
- 41%
- 61%
- 64%
- 59%

Able to name the first five books of the Bible
- 37%
- 48%
- 42%
- 43%

*Ruth was not offered as an option.

than older adults on each of the literacy questions. This highlights one of the consistent themes of *The Bible in America* research: The sacred canopy of the Scriptures does not provide as much shade to the younger generations of Americans, especially the Millennials.

BIBLICAL LITERACY WITHIN THE CHURCH

Younger generations of practicing Christians keep pace with older adults.

PRACTICING CHRISTIANS

	% ALL PRACTICING CHRISTIANS	% MILLENNIALS	% GEN-XERS	% BOOMERS	% ELDERS
Genesis is the name of first book in Bible	88	80	90	89	85
The "3" in John 3:16 is the chapter	77	70	81	80	65
Identify book named after a woman: Esther*	75	59	79	79	67
The name of Abraham's son was Isaac	71	68	76	72	62
The apostle Paul was also known as Saul	69	68	62	72	75
The original language of Old Testament is Hebrew	65	62	67	65	62
The first five books of Bible correctly named	60	60	70	59	49
The name of King David's son was Solomon	58	60	64	56	49
The name of John the Baptist's mother: Elizabeth	46	30	41	53	49
Identify statement found in Bible: The truth will set you free	38	40	42	39	33
The original language of New Testament is Greek	37	31	42	37	31

*Ruth was not offered as an option.

Looking at biblical literacy *within* the Christian community reveals some important insights. First, there is a wide range of knowledge about the Bible that practicing Christians know and do not know. Depending on one's point of view, the findings in the chart represent either good news or bad—or some of both. Nearly nine out of 10 practicing Christians know that Genesis is the first book in the Bible. Is it good news that 88 percent know this basic fact? Or bad news that one in eight does *not*?

One bit of good news comes in the form of generational comparisons among Christians. In contrast to their peers, Bible literacy among practicing Christian Millennials and Gen-Xers is strong. That is, the decline in Bible literacy among Millennials is largely happening *outside* the Christian community, rather than among practicing Christian young adults. There are a few areas in which Millennial Christians are slightly lower than their fellow believers, but these differences are within the range of sampling error.

This research challenges the assumption that younger Christians are less biblically literate than previous generations of Christians. For the most part, where believers maintain Bible literacy, they do so across generations. And where Christians lack Bible knowledge—such as that the New Testament was written in Greek—the deficit is reflected across all the age groups.

THIS RESEARCH CHALLENGES THE ASSUMPTION THAT YOUNGER CHRISTIANS ARE LESS BIBLICALLY LITERATE THAN PREVIOUS GENERATIONS OF CHRISTIANS

7 THE GOOD BOOK IN A DIGITAL CONTEXT

The digital revolution has affected many dimensions of society, including perceptions of and access to religious content. And the research shows clear signs of the revolution when it comes to the Bible in America.

Still, as the most distributed book in history, the vast majority of American households have at least one print Bible, and most

DOES YOUR HOUSEHOLD OWN A BIBLE?

	2011	2012	2013	2014	2015	2016
yes	88	85	88	88	88	86
no	12	15	12	12	13	14

HOW MANY BIBLES, IN TOTAL, DOES YOUR HOUSEHOLD OWN?

% among U.S. adults who own a Bible	2011	2012	2013	2014	2015	2016
mean	4.5	4.3	4.4	4.7	4.4	4.6
median	3.4	3.3	3.5	3.4	3.0	3.0

own more than one. Nearly nine out of 10 U.S. adults report there is a Bible at home, and this proportion is holding steady. The median number of household Bible is 3.0, down slightly over the past six years from 3.4. Even in a digitized world, the Bible is the most ubiquitous book in America.

Americans continue to own Bibles—but is readership as ubiquitous as ownership? No. About one-third of Americans reads the Bible at least once a week, and this proportion has remained fairly stable over the past six years. Likewise, the two out of five U.S. adults who read the Bible less than once a year or never has proven thus far to be a stable proportion. Unless something dramatically changes among Millennials, however, Barna researchers expect reading frequency in the general population to trend downward in coming years as Elders become a smaller share of the total: Half of Elders read the Bible at least once a week (49%), compared to just one-quarter of Millennials (24%).

Nine out of 10 Bible readers—those who report reading the Bible at least three or four times a year—say they have read from a print version or heard the Bible read aloud in a worship service or Mass. About half (a fairly consistent percentage since 2011) say they have studied the Bible in a small group.

Yet as digital devices have proliferated in recent years, so has the availability of the Bible in formats other than print. In a relatively short time, use of tablets and smartphones for Bible searches has skyrocketed, from 18 percent in 2011 to 43 percent in 2016—a 25-point increase. Using the Internet to read the Bible has increased by 12 percentage points since 2011 and listening to a Bible podcast has jumped 13 points. One-third of Bible readers have accessed the Bible through a Bible app.

Among adults who increased their Bible reading over the previous year, one-quarter says the increase was due to having downloaded the Bible to their smartphone or tablet (26%). More than one in eight credits their increased Bible use to podcasts or streaming church services (12%).

All that said, a strong majority still prefers to read the Bible in print (81%). The same holds true even among Millennials (78%), who are most likely to use the Internet to read Bible content (62% vs. 49% of all adults).

The growing popularity of digital technologies represents an enormous opportunity for those who seek to increase Bible engagement—especially among Millennial Bible readers, who are most likely to report using digital versions of the Bible. And while they're just as likely as Gen-Xers and Boomers to express a preference for print, 18 percent say they prefer a smartphone or tablet app—making them twice as likely as Boomers (9%) and six times more likely than Elders (3%) to say so.

THE GROWING POPULARITY OF DIGITAL TECHNOLOGIES REPRESENTS AN ENORMOUS OPPORTUNITY TO INCREASE BIBLE ENGAGEMENT

FORMATS USED WITHIN THE PAST YEAR

% among Bible readers	2011	2012	2013	2014	2015	2016
Read from a print version of the Bible on your own	89	89	90	89	93	92
Heard the Bible read in a worship service or mass					83	90
Attended a small group or Bible study, where you study the Bible in a group, not including weekend worship services	53	47	44	44	53	54
Used the Internet on a computer to read Bible content	37	38	41	44	50	49
Searched for Bible verses or Bible content on a smartphone or cell phone	18	23	29	35	40	43
Listened to a teaching about the Bible via podcast	24	26	26	29	30	37
Downloaded or used a Bible app on a smartphone					35	36
Listened to an audio version of the Bible	28	30	26	25	32	35

Blank fields represent questions that were not tracked 2011–2014.

BIBLE FORMATS USED BY GENERATIONS

% among U.S. Bible readers 18 and older

● Millennials　● Gen-Xers　● Boomers　● Elders

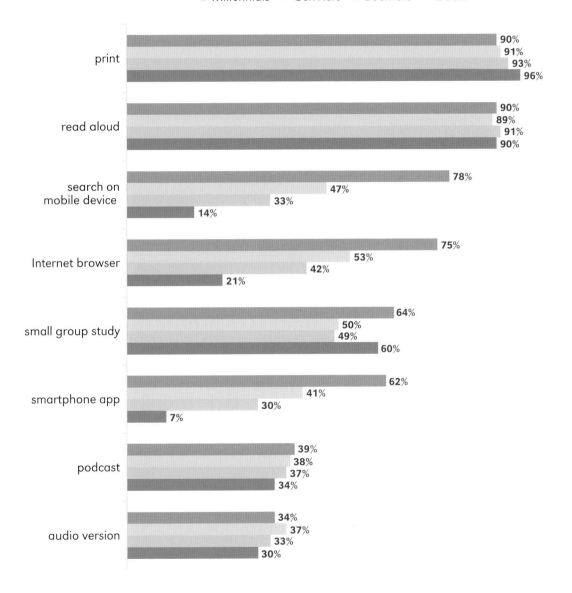

print
- 90%
- 91%
- 93%
- 96%

read aloud
- 90%
- 89%
- 91%
- 90%

search on mobile device
- 78%
- 47%
- 33%
- 14%

Internet browser
- 75%
- 53%
- 42%
- 21%

small group study
- 64%
- 50%
- 49%
- 60%

smartphone app
- 62%
- 41%
- 30%
- 7%

podcast
- 39%
- 38%
- 37%
- 34%

audio version
- 34%
- 37%
- 33%
- 30%

8 THE RISE OF BIBLE SKEPTICS

The data collected by American Bible Society and Barna is evidence of the growing culture of skepticism mentioned in the Introduction. One of the most significant trends revealed by six years of data tracking is the rise of Bible skeptics—that is, people who believe there is no God behind the Bible. These are individuals who believe the Bible is just a book written by men, and who generally draw negative conclusions about the Bible's role in society (for instance, that it is a book used to oppress people, that it powers religious extremism, and so on).

In 2011, when "State of the Bible" tracking began, just 10 percent of American adults qualified as Bible skeptics. In 2016, the proportion has grown to 22 percent of adults—more than doubling in the last half-dozen years. This mirrors the other changes in American religious life, including the rise of the so-called "nones," or religiously unaffiliated.

There are several puzzle pieces needed to complete an accurate picture of skepticism. First, while the Bible remains the top choice among U.S. adults who are asked to identify sacred literature, the

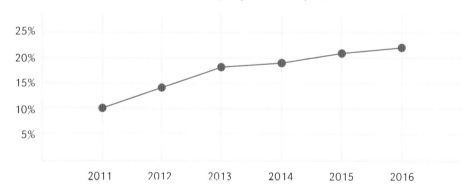

THE RISE OF BIBLE SKEPTICS

% of adults who qualify as Bible skeptics

proportion that chooses the Bible has softened. More telling, the percentage of Americans who opt for "none of these" has doubled in six years, from 7 percent in 2011 to 14 percent in 2016. This increase is mostly thanks to Millennials (22%) and Gen-Xers (18%), who are significantly more likely than Boomers (8%) and Elders (7%) to say none of the options qualifies as a holy book.

Similarly, there is rising skepticism about the Bible as a sufficient guide for living a meaningful life. The percentage of people who strongly agree with the statement has contracted in six years from 53 percent in 2011 to 45 percent in 2016—and the percentages of those who disagree strongly or somewhat have increased over the same time period, from 23 to 33 percent

Here again, there are significant differences between generations. Only 27 percent of all Millennials and 40 percent of Gen-Xers believe the Bible is sufficient for meaningful living—a sea change from the 56 percent of Boomers and two-thirds of Elders (65%) who trust the sufficiency of the Bible.

THERE IS RISING SKEPTICISM ABOUT THE BIBLE AS A SUFFICIENT GUIDE FOR LIVING A MEANINGFUL LIFE

INDICATORS OF BIBLE SKEPTICISM

% of U.S. adults	2011	2012	2013	2014	2015	2016
The Bible is considered sacred	86	82	80	79	79	80
No literature is considered sacred	7	11	12	13	13	14
Percent of adults who qualify as Bible skeptics	10	14	17	19	21	22
Bible contains everything a person needs to know to live a meaningful life (disagree)	23	27	31	30	30	33

Trust in the Bible's reliability is also dropping. Barna first asked U.S. adults in 1991 if they agreed or disagreed that "the Bible is totally accurate in all of the principles it teaches." Twenty-five years ago, 46 percent strongly agreed—close to half—but today, one-third of Americans says so. And the percentage of those who strongly disagree has nearly doubled in six years.

The national shifts in these three perceptions—the Bible is sacred literature, is sufficient as a guide for meaningful living and is reliably accurate—are the clearest indicators that skepticism about the Bible is gaining a stronger cultural foothold. But they are not the only signs. As we'll see in Part IV, non-Christian Millennials—a group that is steadily growing as more of them choose "none" when it comes to religion—are particularly disenchanted with the Bible. Their top descriptors for the Christian Scriptures are "story" (50%), "mythology" (38%), "symbolic" (36%) and "fairy tale" (30%). And more than one-quarter agrees "the Bible is a dangerous book of religious dogma" (27%).

The overall trends are clear: Skepticism toward the Bible is a minority report—for now. But questions about whether the Bible is supernatural and if it produces good things are gaining traction, and demand a response from the Christian community.

QUESTIONS ABOUT WHETHER THE BIBLE IS SUPERNATURAL AND IF IT PRODUCES GOOD THINGS ARE GAINING TRACTION

9 WHAT COMPELS OR PREVENTS ENGAGEMENT?

In an era of significant change, when so many cultural touchstones are up for grabs, what compels people to read an ancient document, or prevents them from reading it? When it comes to reasons people read the Bible, a relatively consistent majority does so because it draws them close to God—but significant minorities in 2016 also point to a need for comfort (16%) or direction (16%). A majority, about six in 10 U.S. adults, also expresses a desire to read the Bible more than they currently do. This desire is another window of opportunity for leaders who care about increasing Bible engagement. And the "felt needs" people bring to Bible reading are also an opportunity to help them engage more deeply with the Scriptures. (For more on these opportunities, read "When Life Stops Making Sense" on page 63.)

MOTIVATIONS FOR READING THE BIBLE

The following are reasons why someone might read the Bible. Please indicate which is most true for you.

% among Bible readers	2011	2012	2013	2014	2015	2016
It brings me closer to God	64	55	53	56	60	55
I need comfort	14	10	14	15	12	16
I have a problem I need to solve or I need direction	12	17	18	17	18	16
I know I'm supposed to	3	5	6	4	4	6
It is part of my studies at school	3	3	4	3	3	3
not sure / none	4	9	12	4	4	4

DESIRE TO READ THE BIBLE

Do you wish that you read the Bible more or not?

% among U.S. adults	2011	2012	2013	2014	2015	2016
yes	67	60	61	62	61	61
no	31	38	37	36	38	36
don't know	2	2	2	2	1	3

MOST PEOPLE'S BIBLE READING IS STABLE

Would you say that your own personal use of the Bible has increased, decreased or is about the same as one year ago?

% among U.S. adults	2012	2013	2014	2015	2016
stayed the same	58	63	71	66	66
increased	27	26	18	22	23
decreased	12	9	9	12	8
not sure	3	2	1	1	3

About one-quarter of Americans says their Bible use increased since one year ago, and two-thirds report it stayed about the same during that time. Among those who experienced an increase, most attribute their growing use of the Bible to a realization that the Scriptures are an important part of their faith journey (67%). One in four says they have been through a difficult experience that prompted them to turn to the Bible (26%), and one in five reports a significant change, such as marriage or the birth of a child, that inspired an increase in Bible use (20%). (Keep in mind these are respondents' *perceptions* of the barriers to Bible reading.)

What keeps people from reading the Bible? Like other forms of analog media, the Bible is pushed to the side in part because people are too busy. Among those who say their Bible reading decreased in the last year, the number one reason was busyness: Nearly six in 10 report being too busy with life's responsibilities (job, family, etc.), an increase of 18 points since 2014 (58% vs. 40%).

Other factors Americans cite as reasons for less time reading the Scriptures include becoming atheist or agnostic (17%), going through a difficult experience that caused them to doubt

WHAT COMPELS GREATER BIBLE ENGAGEMENT?

What do you think caused the increase in your Bible engagement?

% who experienced an increase in engagement; multiple response

Came to understand it as an important part of my faith journey	67
Difficult experience in my life caused me to search the Bible for direction / answers	26
Significant change in my life (marriage, birth of child, etc.)	20
Downloaded the Bible onto my smartphone or tablet	18
Saw how the Bible changed someone I know for the better	14
Went to a church where the Bible became more accessible to me	12
Someone I know asked me to read the Bible with them	10
Media conversations around religion and spirituality	5
other	12

God (12%) or experiencing a significant change such as a job loss or death in the family (8%). These relatively smaller percentages reveal that people don't often turn away from the Bible over ideological or emotional conflicts. Indeed, on the whole Americans say they *want* to read the Bible—again, two-thirds wish they read the Scriptures more—they just don't know how to make time.

PEOPLE DON'T OFTEN TURN AWAY FROM THE BIBLE OVER IDEOLOGICAL OR EMOTIONAL CONFLICTS

Taken together, the trends indicated by the data are toward growing skepticism and diminishing Bible engagement across the U.S. population. Yet, as Part III reveals, there are demographic segments within the overall population that buck those trends. Swimming against the cultural tide of religious indifference and suspicion of authority, committed people of faith in every age and ethnic group continue to trust God's word as reliable and authoritative for their lives and for the Church.

When Life Stops Making Sense

Why do people read the Bible?

More than half of Bible readers (55%) say the main reason is that it brings them closer to God. On another question, of the 23 percent of readers whose Bible reading increased in the past year, two-thirds say it was because they "came to understand it as an important part of my faith journey."

Here we get a great picture of a substantial group of Bible readers, people with a growing faith, progressing in their journey, getting closer to God with every chapter. This is the majority report.

But there's a smaller group worth mentioning. When asked for their main reason for reading the Bible, 16 percent of readers say they need comfort, and another 16 percent say, "I have a problem I need to solve or I need direction." On the question about reasons for increasing their reading, about one-quarter say, "A difficult experience in my life caused me to search the Bible for direction / answers."

So, while a slight majority of Bible readers come from a positive place, depending on the Bible to continue their spiritual growth, nearly one-third are coming from a place of need. They need comfort. They have problems to solve. They need direction.

Scripture works both ways. Psalm 1 gives us an image of happy people who "find joy in obeying the law of the Lord, and they study it day and night" (v. 2). But flip over to Psalm 73 for a different take:

> God is indeed good to Israel,
>> to those who have pure hearts.
> But I had nearly lost confidence;
>> my faith was almost gone.
>> (Ps. 73:1–2)

RANDY PETERSEN

Randy Petersen works with American Bible Society as Director of Scripture Engagement Resources. Author of more than 60 books, he has also written Bible study curriculum for RightNow Media, David C. Cook and Mainstay Church Resources. Randy teaches often and preaches occasionally at Hope United Methodist Church of Voorhees, New Jersey, where he also serves on the leadership team. His latest book, *The Printer and the Preacher*, focuses on the friendship between Great Awakening preacher George Whitefield and Benjamin Franklin.

That psalm goes on to complain about the success of the wicked and the difficulty of living for God. Life may be great for the 55 percent, and God is good to the pure-hearted, but as for *me*—well, it's a very different story. I have problems and struggles. I suffer. Sometimes I feel God is punishing me.

Both Sides Now

Any attempt to promote Bible engagement needs to take both the majority and the minority position into account. We need to cheer on those who are moving forward in their faith journey, growing steadily closer to God as they read the Bible. But we also need to bring the word of God into the troubled reality of those who are in need.

There's one category in the survey that jumps out and confirms this point. "Non-practicing Christians" call themselves Christian but don't go to church even once a month. When asked to choose one statement that would explain their motivation for reading the Bible, only 35 percent say, "It brings me closer to God" (far below the overall 55%). But combining the "I need comfort" (29%) and "I have a problem . . ." (23%) answers, *we find more than half of non-practicing Christians coming to the Scriptures from a place of need.*

And that makes sense. These people are not joining in regular worship and fellowship at church. They don't receive that weekly support in their faith journey. They aren't Psalm 1 people, studying the Bible "day and night." They might be Psalm 73 people—dealing with difficult questions and doubts. For them, God's word is not daily bread as much as a lifeline.

Tough Times

Fortunately, the Bible is no stranger to tough times. From Joseph to Job to Jeremiah to Jesus, we find people facing difficult circumstances. Dozens of psalms are full of lament. "How long, Lord, how long?" is a theme common to the prophets, as well (see, for example, Habakkuk 1:2; Zechariah 1:12; Psalm 6:3). Jesus warned his followers to expect trouble (see John 16:33), and Paul wrote passionately about all of creation "groaning" as we await God's redemption (see Romans 8:22).

For those who come to the Scriptures from a situation of need—well, they've come to the right place. The problem is, they might be looking for the wrong kind of solution. Our consumer culture teaches us to treat every problem with a quick fix. Some bring that approach to Bible reading. *Grab some comfort. Get an answer. Here's a verse that will cure what ails you.*

And *sometimes* the Bible works like that. It's a powerful book. The Spirit of God blows through its pages and works all sorts of miracles. But the Lord wants more from this encounter. He wants to build a relationship with us.

Shattered

When people experience serious trauma, certain assumptions are shattered. We tend to go through life assuming we have value in a world that is orderly and fair. But then there's a random act of violence, a betrayal, a natural disaster that causes injury or loss—and we have to re-examine everything. Is there order in the world or only chaos? Is there justice, or will good people keep suffering? Am I loved and valued by other people and by God?

These questions shake us to the core. They add emotional and spiritual turmoil to whatever physical and relational pain we feel. Some people run to the Bible as a way to shore up those original assumptions. But wiser ones *crawl into* the Bible and live there for a while. They don't just grab a verse; they get the big story.

That story is found throughout the Scriptures, in many forms. It recognizes that this world is fallen and redemption is a rocky road. Some mysteries remain; some questions go unanswered. Yes, "all of creation groans with pain" as it decays into disorder, and we groan with it (Rom. 8:19–23). Yet our God is taking the injustices of the world and refashioning a good outcome for those who love him (see Romans 8:28; Genesis 50:20). We may have to endure "hardship or persecution or hunger or poverty or danger or death" but none of it can "separate us from the love of Christ" (Rom. 8:35–37).

These aren't "Bible Band-Aids," covering deep wounds with surface platitudes. These passages go to the core of God's relationship with this world. As people take the time to engage fully with God's word, they get more than answers. They get healing.

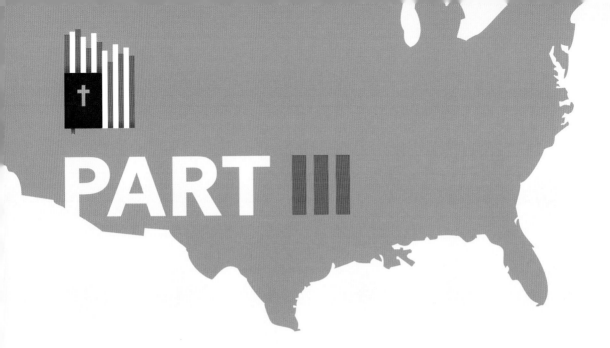

PART III

THE BIBLE AMONG KEY DEMOGRAPHICS

As we've seen, older adults are more likely than Gen-Xers and Millennials to engage with the Scriptures, but differences in Bible beliefs and practices crop up between other population segments, too. When researchers group people together according to faith practice or Christian tradition, or by ethnic identification, variations emerge.

Part III parses the Barna-American Bible Society data along key demographic lines. A few things to notice:

- Practicing Christians maintain strong beliefs and robust reading habits when it comes to the Bible.
- Catholics and Hispanic Americans read the Bible less frequently than other groups, but engage with the Scriptures in other ways.
- African Americans tend to be highly engaged with the Bible, maintaining "high" views of the Scriptures and reading them more often than white and Hispanic adults.

PRACTICING CHRISTIANS AND THE BIBLE

Barna defines "practicing Christians" as self-identified Christians who say their faith is very important in their lives and who have attended a worship service within the past month. These folks make up about one-third of the total U.S. adult population.

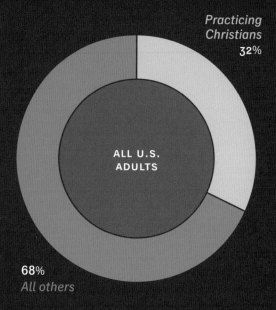

Practicing Christians **32%**

ALL U.S. ADULTS

68% *All others*

BY GENERATION

Regardless of generation, practicing Christians tend to have both higher views of Scripture and more frequent Bible reading habits than the U.S. norm.

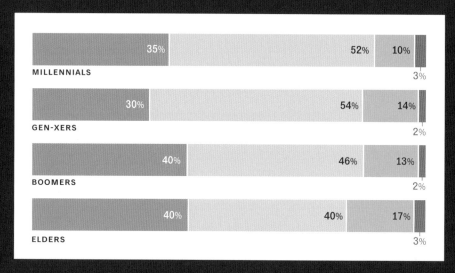

⊕ *Bible Engaged*
⊕ *Bible Friendly*
⊖ *Bible Neutral*
⊖ *Bible Skeptic*

MILLENNIALS
35%   52%   10%   3%

GEN-XERS
30%   54%   14%   2%

BOOMERS
40%   46%   13%   2%

ELDERS
40%   40%   17%   3%

BY FAITH TRADITION

Practicing Christians come from a variety of faith traditions.
The largest of these are Catholic, mainline and non-mainline,
a category that includes such denominations as Southern Baptist,
Assemblies of God and other Pentecostal or Charismatic churches,
and non-denominational congregations. Non-mainline attenders
make up the largest share of practicing Christians.

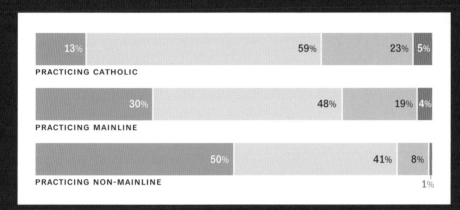

+	Bible Engaged		
+	Bible Friendly		
−	Bible Neutral		
−	Bible Skeptic		

PRACTICING CATHOLIC: 13% · 59% · 23% · 5%

PRACTICING MAINLINE: 30% · 48% · 19% · 4%

PRACTICING NON-MAINLINE: 50% · 41% · 8% · 1%

BY ETHNICITY

Ethnicity also seems to be a factor in Bible engagement:
Black Americans are more likely than whites and Hispanics to
be *engaged*, and less likely to be *skeptics*. (They are also more likely
to be practicing Christians.)

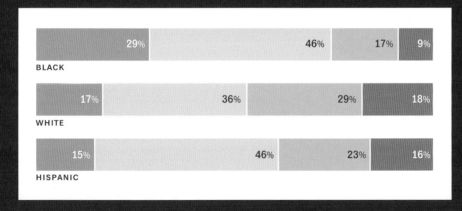

+	Bible Engaged		
+	Bible Friendly		
−	Bible Neutral		
−	Bible Skeptic		

BLACK: 29% · 46% · 17% · 9%

WHITE: 17% · 36% · 29% · 18%

HISPANIC: 15% · 46% · 23% · 16%

Barna / American Bible Society 2011–2016, *N*=12,062. Totals may not equal 100 percent due to rounding.

10 PRACTICING CHRISTIANS

A majority of Americans chooses "Christian" when asked to identify their religion. Most of these self-identified Christians, however, do not consider their faith a high priority or regularly attend church. Only about one-third of the total U.S. population is a "practicing Christian," who say their faith is very important and attended at least one worship service within the past month.

When it comes to beliefs about the Bible, practicing Christians are quite different from adults who do not practice Christianity (including those who identify as Christian). They are twice as likely as other adults to choose one of the top two "high" views of the Bible (81% vs. 41%), and nine out of 10 say it is either the actual or the inspired word of God (91%).

a. **The actual word of God** and should be taken literally, word for word

b. The inspired word of God and has no errors, although some verses are meant to be symbolic rather than literal

c. The inspired word of God but has some factual or historical errors

d. Not inspired by God but tells how the writers of the Bible understood the ways and principles of God

e. Just another book of teaching written by men that contains stories and advice

f. Other / don't know

THE BEST DEFINITION OF THE BIBLE:
PRACTICING CHRISTIANS VS. ALL OTHER U.S. ADULTS

% among U.S. adults 18 and older

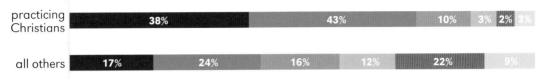

practicing Christians	38%	43%	10%	3%	2%	3%
all others	17%	24%	16%	12%	22%	9%

Practicing Christians are also more likely than other Americans to say the Bible contains everything one needs to know in order to live a meaningful life (90% vs. 57% among adults who do not practice Christianity).

As one might expect, those who practice their Christian faith read the Bible more than other adults—much more, in fact. Seven in 10 report reading the Scriptures at least once a week—more than three times the percentage of other Americans (22%)—and three in 10 say they read every day. There are some ethnic, generational and denominational differences among practicing Christians, however, which are examined in later section.

7 OUT OF 10 PRACTICING CHRISTIANS READ THE BIBLE AT LEAST ONCE A WEEK

HOW FREQUENTLY AMERICANS READ THE BIBLE:
PRACTICING CHRISTIANS VS. ALL OTHER U.S. ADULTS

% among U.S. adults 18 and older

● every day   ● once/week   ● 1-2 times year
● 4+ times/week   ● once/month   ● < once/year
● several times/week ● 3-4 times/year   ● never

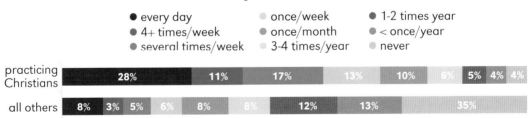

practicing Christians	28%	11%	17%	13%	10%	6%	5%	4%	4%
all others	8%	3%	5%	6%	8%	8%	12%	13%	35%

Combining Bible belief and reading habits, we find that practicing Christians are much more likely than those who do not practice the faith to be Bible engaged (37% vs. 9%) or Bible friendly (47% vs. 33%).

BIBLE ENGAGEMENT IN AMERICA:
PRACTICING CHRISTIANS VS. ALL OTHER U.S. ADULTS
% among U.S. adults 18 and older

● Bible engaged   ● Bible friendly   ● Bible neutral   ● Bible skeptic

	Bible engaged	Bible friendly	Bible neutral	Bible skeptic
practicing Christians	37%	47%	13%	3%
all others	9%	33%	33%	25%

Within the practicing Christian community there are some differences between the generations, but overall this group stands in stark contrast to their age cohorts in the general population. In Part IV we take a closer look at generational differences among all U.S. teens and adults and among practicing Christians.

11 CATHOLICS

Practicing Catholics—who say their faith is very important in their life and have attended Mass within the past month—seem, at first glance, to engage less with the Bible than other practicing Christians. But it may be more accurate to say they engage *differently*.

When it comes to beliefs about the Bible, practicing Catholics (86%) are much more likely than the national average (68%) and non-practicing Catholics (68%) to hold an orthodox view that it is the actual or inspired word of God.

a. **The actual word of God** and should be taken literally, word for word

b. The inspired word of God and has no errors, although some verses are meant to be symbolic rather than literal

c. The inspired word of God **but has some factual or historical errors**

d. Not inspired by God **but tells how the writers of the Bible understood the ways and principles of God**

e. **Just another book of teaching written by men that contains stories and advice**

f. Other / don't know

THE BEST DEFINITION OF THE BIBLE: PRACTICING CATHOLICS

% among U.S. adults 18 and older

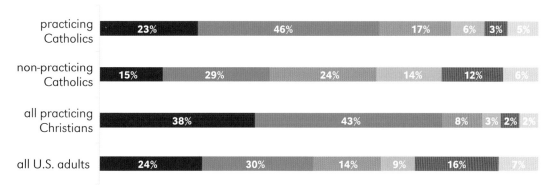

practicing Catholics	23%	46%	17%	6%	3%	5%
non-practicing Catholics	15%	29%	24%	14%	12%	6%
all practicing Christians	38%	43%	8%	3%	2%	2%
all U.S. adults	24%	30%	14%	9%	16%	7%

Barna defines "Bible readers" as people who report reading the Scriptures at least three to four times a year. Under this definition, two-thirds of practicing Catholics (64%) are Bible readers, compared to just over half of all U.S. adults (54%) and just one-third of non-practicing Catholics (32%). Nearly nine out of 10 practicing Christians overall—a group that includes both Catholics and Protestants—are Bible readers (86%), which indicates that more practicing Protestants than practicing Catholics read the Bible three or four times a year or more.

Practicing Catholics read the Bible less frequently than practicing Christians as a whole, but they *hear* the Bible read aloud about as often as all practicing Christians. Nine out of 10

PRACTICING CATHOLICS SEEM TO ENGAGE LESS WITH THE BIBLE THAN OTHER PRACTICING CHRISTIANS—BUT IT MAY BE MORE ACCURATE TO SAY THEY ENGAGE *DIFFERENTLY*

practicing Catholics (91%) hear the Bible at least monthly, which is on par with all practicing Christians (94%) and nearly three times as often as non-practicing Catholics (35%).

In addition, two out of five practicing Catholics (39%) report reading the Scriptures within the past week in a liturgical text such as the Liturgy of the Hours or a *Lectio Divina* resource. This is a greater percentage than among all practicing Christians (31%), non-practicing Catholics (3%) and U.S. adults overall (18%).

BIBLE READERS: PRACTICING CATHOLICS
% among U.S. adults 18 and older

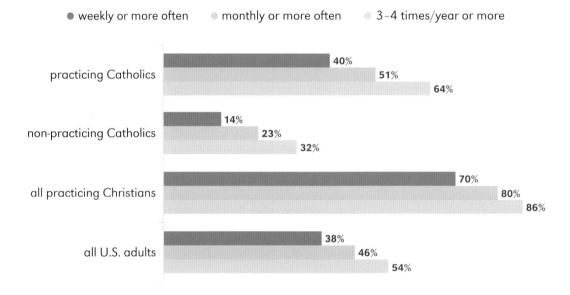

● weekly or more often   ● monthly or more often   ● 3–4 times/year or more

practicing Catholics
- 40%
- 51%
- 64%

non-practicing Catholics
- 14%
- 23%
- 32%

all practicing Christians
- 70%
- 80%
- 86%

all U.S. adults
- 38%
- 46%
- 54%

Q&A WITH **SIR MARIO PAREDES**

Q: The American Bible Society was founded by Protestants 200 years ago. In the last few decades, however, many Catholics have connected with American Bible Society's mission and have been working with and in the organization. How do you see Protestants and Catholics coming together to accomplish this mission?

A: American Bible Society carries forward its mission to distribute God's word in the Bible without proselytism or dogmatism; not as a platform to defend Protestantism in the world; not to promote, defend or attack doctrinal postures—but as a service to the world to aid in the enlightenment of human life and the unity of the mystical Body of Christ through the knowledge, study and propagation of the Bible, which is the foundation of the Christian faith.

The outreach of American Bible Society to Catholics came in the wake of the Vatican II Ecumenical Council, which emphasized the centrality of the word of God in the life and activity of the Catholic Church. Now Catholic and Protestant work together for the fulfillment of Jesus' desire: "That they all might be one" (John 17:20). This desire, this disposition, has become the task of the Church, of every person and community in all the world that believes in Christ: that we all might become *one*, as the Father and the Son are *one*.

Jesus' desire defines the ecumenical task of Christian churches in the world. And this ecumenism is embodied in the collaboration between different churches and denominations to publish, distribute, present, promote and offer encounters with the sacred Scriptures.

▼

SIR MARIO PAREDES

Mario J. Paredes, K.G.C.H.S., is a member of American Bible Society's Board of Trustees and former Director of ABS Catholic Ministries. He is Founder and Chairman Emeritus of the Board for Catholic Association of Latino Leaders (CALL) and serves as president of the North American-Chilean Chamber of Commerce of New York and vice president of Gabriela Mistral Foundation.

He was created Knight Grand Cross of the Equestrian Order of the Holy Sepulchre of Jerusalem in 2012.

Q: What are some of the specific ways American Bible Society is working with and in the Catholic Church?

A: American Bible Society collaborated in the Synod of the Catholic Church on the Bible, in which Dr. Dennis Dickerson, former president of the Board of Trustees, and I participated as observers. In the solemnity of that occasion, American Bible Society donated to the Catholic Church a special edition of 1,000 copies of the Polyglot Bible (in five languages: Hebrew, Greek, Latin, English and Spanish) for distribution among the Synodal Fathers and as gifts presented by the Pope in audiences with heads of state and other high-level dignitaries.

The flagship program of the ecumenical and interconfessional task has, in recent years, been *Lectio Divina*, the methodology by which the word of God is read and reflected upon in prayer. Through the partnership of American Bible Society and Libreria Editrice Vaticana (the Vatican editorial house), a manual for practicing *Lectio Divina* has been published in three languages: English, Spanish and Italian.

American Bible Society has been present in worldwide youth activities organized by the Vatican in Madrid, Rio de Janeiro and soon Krakow to distribute the Bible and resources to young Catholic attendees. The organization also presented a petition, which was approved last year by the National Conference of Catholic Bishops, to celebrate a nationwide annual Week of the Bible for Catholics.

American Bible Society participated in the 2015 World Meeting of Families in Philadelphia by partnering with the Pontifical Council for the Family to develop a polyglot edition of the Gospel of St. Luke, of which half a million copies were distributed. This special edition features a dedication by Pope Francis, a foreword by Archbishop Charles Chaput of Philadelphia and an introduction by Archbishop Vincenzo Paglia, President of the Pontifical Council for the Family. In addition, American Bible Society created a series of biblical messages supporting the World Meeting of Families.

The effort concerning the written word of God that motivates the daily activity of American Bible Society is a magnificent testimony and beautiful evidence of the evangelizing zeal, both ecclesial and personal, that every Christian should assume in the fulfillment of the command of our divine Master: "Go throughout the whole world and preach the gospel to all people" (Mark 16:15).

12 HISPANIC AMERICANS*

Fifteen percent of Hispanic Americans qualify as Bible engaged, which is slightly below the national average of 18 percent. They are more likely than the U.S. norm, however, to be Bible friendly (46% vs. 38%). They are less engaged than average not because of belief—in fact, they are more likely to hold a "high" view of the Scriptures, as seen below—but because fewer Hispanics report reading the Bible every day (12% vs. 14% among all U.S. adults) or multiple times per week (4% vs. 5%).

In general, Hispanic Americans have a high opinion of the Bible: Seven in 10 (72%) say that it is the actual or inspired word of God, and more than half (59%) believe it is true in all it teaches. In fact, on both counts Hispanics actually have a "higher" view of the Scriptures than is true of non-Hispanic Americans. And the non-Christian Hispanic population maintains more respect toward the origins and authority of the Bible than is true among other non-Christians in the U.S.

HOW FREQUENTLY AMERICANS READ THE BIBLE: HISPANICS VS. ALL U.S. ADULTS

% among U.S. adults 18 and older

- every day
- 4+ times/week
- several times/week
- once/week
- once/month
- 3-4 times/year
- 1-2 times year
- < once/year
- never

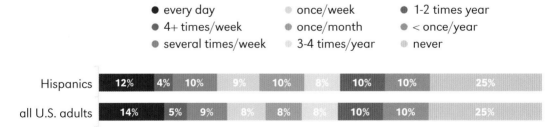

	every day	4+ times/week	several times/week	once/week	once/month	3-4 times/year	1-2 times year	< once/year	never
Hispanics	12%	4%	10%	9%	10%	8%	10%	10%	25%
all U.S. adults	14%	5%	9%	8%	8%	8%	10%	10%	25%

Hispanic America: Faith, Values and Priorities (Barna, 2012) is a collaboration of Barna Group, American Bible Society, The National Hispanic Christian Leadership Conference and OneHope.

THE BEST DEFINITION OF THE BIBLE: HISPANICS VS. ALL U.S. ADULTS

% among U.S. adults 18 and older

a. **The actual word of God** and should be taken literally, word for word

b. **The inspired word of God and has no errors,** although some verses are meant to be symbolic rather than literal

c. The inspired word of God **but has some factual or historical errors**

d. Not inspired by God **but tells how the writers of the Bible understood the ways and principles of God**

e. **Just another book of teaching written by men that contains stories and advice**

f. Other / don't know

Are Hispanic Americans really less Bible engaged than the overall U.S. population? In fact, by controlling for denominational differences, Hispanic Protestants (31%) are statistically on par with non-Hispanic Protestants (29%) when it comes to being Bible engaged. Among Catholics, whether they are Hispanic (8% engaged) or non-Hispanic (7%), Bible engagement tends to be lower. So the real differences lie not in ethnicity per se, but in religious affiliation. Hispanics (68%) are more likely than the general population (19%) to be Catholic, and Catholics overall are less likely to be Bible engaged.

HISPANICS ARE MORE LIKELY THAN THE GENERAL POPULATION TO BE CATHOLIC, AND CATHOLICS OVERALL ARE LESS LIKELY TO BE BIBLE ENGAGED

THE BIBLE'S INFLUENCE ON U.S. SOCIETY: HISPANICS VS. ALL U.S. ADULTS

% among U.S. adults 18 and older

● too little ● just right ● too much ● don't know

	too little	just right	too much	don't know
Hispanics	42%	35%	17%	5%
all U.S. adults	51%	28%	16%	5%

When it comes to the intersection of the Bible with culture, Hispanics in America are a bit more skeptical than the general population about the role of the Bible in U.S. society. They are less likely to say it has too little influence on culture (42% vs. 51% among all U.S. adults) and more than one-third say its level of influence is just right (35% vs. 28%).

7 OUT OF 10 HISPANIC AMERICANS BELIEVE THE BIBLE CONTAINS EVERYTHING A PERSON NEEDS TO KNOW TO LIVE A MEANINGFUL LIFE

However, when it comes to believing the sufficiency of the Bible's contents as a guide for meaningful life, Hispanic Americans have a higher opinion than the general population. Seven in 10 agree the Bible contains everything a person needs to know to live a meaningful life (71%), compared to about two-thirds of all Americans (68%).

Most Hispanics don't see the Bible merely as a book of valuable teachings (a view that is becoming more common among the general population); they see it as the very word of God. If anything, Hispanics' high regard for the Scriptures suggests that they could be "tipped" toward Bible engagement more readily than non-Hispanics. The foundation of belief is there. What's missing is a clear understanding of how and why the Bible can generate personal and community transformation.

Q&A WITH **REV. BONNIE CAMARDA**

Q: As a bilingual leader, have you observed differences in how Spanish-speaking and English-speaking Christians engage with the Bible personally or corporately, or both?

A: I have observed that Spanish-speaking Christians tend to display their faith in a more vibrant and open manner than English-speaking Christians. This was very evident during the Pope's visit to Philadelphia—I witnessed thousands of Hispanic Christians marching through the streets holding signs, playing instruments and singing and dancing on their way to Mass. Spanish-speaking Christians, particularly the impoverished, seem to turn naturally to their spirituality to guide them through life's challenges. They tend to be very verbal about their beliefs. That being said, I know Christians of all ethnicities who know the gospel, who are fervent and devoted to the Bible's teachings, whether or not they display it publicly. Regardless of language, engaging with the Bible is so important in urban ministry, because its lessons help us address the root challenges of violence and poverty.

Q: In what ways has your education in theology and biblical studies informed your leadership both inside and outside the church?

A: I was one of the few women in that particular seminary to obtain a graduate degree at the time. I was blessed that the president of the seminary, an 80-year-old man, recognized the need for women in leadership in the next generation. Having him as a mentor helped set me up for success as a leader throughout my life.

In my leadership roles inside and outside the church, I have come to believe that biblical teaching has to go beyond the church walls. We must go out into the community. Christianity should not be centralized within a physical church; rather our faith is about connecting with people in the community and sharing the gospel.

REV. BONNIE CAMARDA

Reverend Bonnie Camarda has been Divisional Director of Partnerships for The Salvation Army of Eastern Pennsylvania and Delaware since 1999. She is at the heart of The Salvation Army's initiatives to form fruitful partnerships with area business leaders, government leaders, prospective donors, fellow social service organizations and individuals looking for spiritual guidance and hope. She has degrees in Business Administration and Administrative Science, as well as a Masters of Divinity. Rev. Camarda is highly involved in her community, and in Hispanic and other faith organizations.

13 AFRICAN AMERICANS

African Americans read the Bible more frequently and hold "higher" views of the Scriptures than whites or Hispanics.

Eight out of 10 black adults (82%) hold an orthodox view of the Bible (that it is the actual or inspired word of God), compared to seven in 10 Hispanics (72%) and two-thirds of whites (67%). Half of black practicing Christians (49%) believe the Bible is the actual word of God, compared to 38 percent of all practicing Christians and just one-quarter of all U.S. adults (24%).

In a similar vein, African Americans report reading the Bible more frequently than Hispanics or whites. More than half of all black adults (55%) say they read the Bible at least once a week, compared to one-third of Hispanics (35%) and whites (34%). Eight out of 10 black practicing Christians (79%) read the Bible once a week or more often, outstripping the larger practicing Christian segment (70%).

8 OUT OF 10 BLACK PRACTICING CHRISTIANS READ THE BIBLE AT LEAST ONCE A WEEK

a. **The actual word of God** and should be taken literally, word for word

b. The inspired word of God and has no errors, although some verses are meant to be symbolic rather than literal

c. The inspired word of God but has some factual or historical errors

d. Not inspired by God but tells how the writers of the Bible understood the ways and principles of God

e. Just another book of teaching written by men that contains stories and advice

f. Other / don't know

THE BEST DEFINITION OF THE BIBLE: ETHNICITY AND FAITH PRACTICE

% among U.S. adults 18 and older

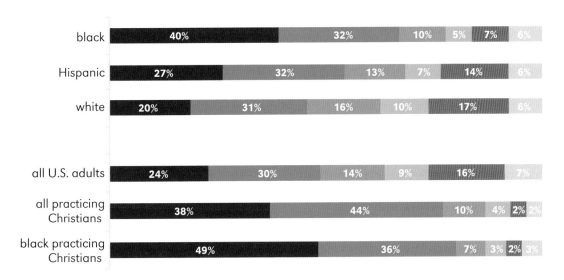

black	40%	32%	10%	5%	7% 6%
Hispanic	27%	32%	13%	7%	14% 6%
white	20%	31%	16%	10%	17% 6%
all U.S. adults	24%	30%	14%	9%	16% 7%
all practicing Christians	38%	44%	10%	4%	2% 2%
black practicing Christians	49%	36%	7%	3%	2% 3%

HOW FREQUENTLY AMERICANS READ THE BIBLE: ETHNICITY

% among U.S. adults 18 and older

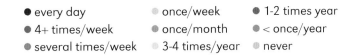

- ● every day
- ● 4+ times/week
- ● several times/week
- ○ once/week
- ● once/month
- ○ 3-4 times/year
- ● 1-2 times year
- ● < once/year
- ● never

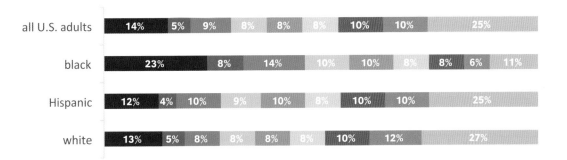

all U.S. adults	14%	5%	9%	8%	8%	8%	10%	10%	25%
black	23%	8%	14%	10%	10%	8%	8%	6%	11%
Hispanic	12%	4%	10%	9%	10%	8%	10%	10%	25%
white	13%	5%	8%	8%	8%	8%	10%	12%	27%

BIBLE ENGAGEMENT IN AMERICA: ETHNICITY
% among U.S. adults 18 and older

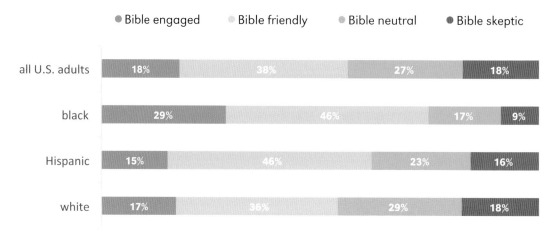

● Bible engaged ● Bible friendly ● Bible neutral ● Bible skeptic

	Bible engaged	Bible friendly	Bible neutral	Bible skeptic
all U.S. adults	18%	38%	27%	18%
black	29%	46%	17%	9%
Hispanic	15%	46%	23%	16%
white	17%	36%	29%	18%

Since black adults read the Bible more often and hold "higher" than average beliefs about the Scriptures, it stands to reason that they tend to be more Bible engaged—and that is indeed the case. They are nearly twice as likely to be Bible engaged (29%) as Hispanics (15%) and whites (17%).

Yet, as Bishop Claude Alexander reveals in an interview with Barna on the following pages, some leaders within the historically Black Church have witnessed a diminishment of the Bible's authority in recent years. The data does not yet reflect this phenomenon; for now, the Bible remains a powerful spiritual icon in the African American community.

Q&A WITH **BISHOP CLAUDE ALEXANDER**

Q: In addition to leading a large church in Charlotte, you are also a civic leader in your community. How do the Scriptures inform your engagement and leadership outside the church?

A: Both the Old and New Testaments speak of God's people exerting a redemptive and sanctifying impact on society. In so doing, a witness is given to God. Through the Word becoming flesh, dwelling among us and revealing the grace and truth of the Father, we are given our example and a challenge to likewise dwell among those in the world and reveal God's grace and truth. As light and salt, we are called to be clarifiers, transformers and preservers. This is done through the good works we do, the love we show, the peace we pursue, the justice we seek, the humility we display, the mercy we extend and the righteousness we exhibit. As Jesus was moved by compassion to bring healing to others, so are we called to restorative action in the world, fueled by compassion.

Q: As the pastor of The Park Church for more than 25 years, how have you seen Bible engagement change in your congregation during that time? Are people more engaged, less engaged or engaged in different ways with the Scriptures than 25 years ago?

A: I have seen a diminishing in the acceptance of the Bible's authority in the hearts and minds of our culture. As a result, the Bible is no longer seen as necessary to people as it once was. With the emergence of secularism and pluralism, which make all claims of truth subjective and equally valid, the Scriptures seem to have less sway.

With that being said, the advent of YouVersion and other Bible apps have made access to the Bible greater than ever before. With

**BISHOP
CLAUDE ALEXANDER**

Bishop Claude Alexander has served as the senior pastor of The Park Church in Charlotte, North Carolina, for 26 years.
A graduate of Morehouse College, Pittsburgh Theological Seminary and Gordon-Conwell Theological Seminary, he has exercised leadership in various civic and religious capacities.
He serves on the boards of Charlotte Center City Partners, Wycliffe Bible Translators USA, *Christianity Today*, the Mission America Coalition and the Joint College of African-American Pentecostal Bishops. He is also the vice chairman of the Gordon-Conwell Board of Trustees.

the access comes a greater possibility of people engaging with the Scriptures.

Q: According to Barna research, many people are "hearers of the Word" rather than "readers of the Word"— that is, they hear the Bible read and preached at church but do not read it on their own. From your long experience in the pulpit, how have you seen the preaching and proclamation of God's word transform people's lives?

A: The preaching of God's word has been and continues to be a means by which many are brought into a saving and transformative relationship with Jesus Christ. Where the word of God is declared, people are challenged to meet the God of the Scriptures in ways that critique, convict, heal, restore, revive and guide them. Also, when pastors preach through a book of the Bible, members are encouraged to increase their reading in preparation for or reflection on the messages that are preached.

The challenge then becomes developing a personal hunger and thirst for the word of God during the week. That is why we use various read-through-the-Bible challenges each year. This year we are using OWNit365 Whole Year Bible Plan.

PART IV

THE BIBLE FOR EVERY GENERATION

As far back as the 1990s, Barna Group's founder, George Barna, was thinking and talking about generational differences. In *The Frog in the Kettle*, published in 1990, he examined the generational views of Elders (born 1945 and before), Boomers (1946 to 1964) and the generation he called "Baby Busters" (1965 to 1983), today more commonly called Gen-X.

In the tradition of George Barna's pioneering work, Barna researchers have continued to observe and document overarching differences between the four adult generations alive in the U.S. today. Part IV takes a closer look at Millennials ages 18 to 31, and at younger teens as well.

Overall, Millennials are less religious and more skeptical than older Americans—and their views on the Bible reflect these tendencies. Yet there is more that unites the four generations than divides them. Barna research confirms the central role this revered text has for most Americans. A majority in each generation believes the Bible is a sacred or holy book. Millions within each age group report reading the Scriptures in the last week.

Despite these similarities, the youngest generations are charting a new course related to the Bible. Here are some of the changes being forged by young adults:

- *Less sacred.* While most people identify the Bible as sacred or holy, the drop-off among Millennials is striking.
- *A negative brand.* Non-Christian Millennials hold ambivalent and sometimes extremely negative views about the Bible.
- *Lower engagement.* The younger the person, the less likely he or she is to read the Bible.

Finally, practicing Christians in each age group are highly engaged with the Bible, and are more similar to each other in their views about the Scriptures than they are to their peers in the general population. Among practicing Christians, fidelity to the Bible remains strong.

I. PRACTICING CHRISTIAN MILLENNIALS: A HIGH VIEW OF SCRIPTURE

THE TOP 5 WORDS PRACTICING CHRISTIAN MILLENNIALS CHOOSE TO DESCRIBE THE BIBLE

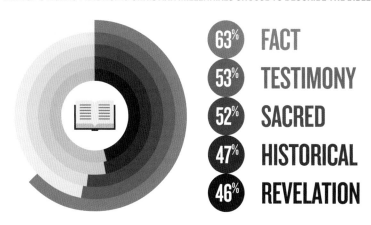

- 63% FACT
- 53% TESTIMONY
- 52% SACRED
- 47% HISTORICAL
- 46% REVELATION

~7 IN 10

THE NUMBER OF PRACTICING CHRISTIAN MILLENNIALS WHO BELIEVE THE BIBLE CONTAINS EVERYTHING A PERSON NEEDS TO KNOW TO LIVE A MEANINGFUL LIFE (69%)

IT IS THEIR TOP SOURCE FOR MORAL TRUTH

39% BIBLE

16% CHURCH

14% PARENTS

THEY BELIEVE IT IS THE ACTUAL WORD OF GOD

35% THE BIBLE IS THE ACTUAL WORD OF GOD AND SHOULD BE TAKEN LITERALLY, WORD FOR WORD

50% THE BIBLE IS THE INSPIRED WORD OF GOD AND HAS NO ERRORS, ALTHOUGH SOME VERSES ARE MEANT TO BE SYMBOLIC RATHER THAN LITERAL

11% THE BIBLE IS THE INSPIRED WORD OF GOD BUT HAS SOME FACTUAL OR HISTORICAL ERRORS

2. NON-CHRISTIAN MILLENNIALS: AMBIVALENT, SOMETIMES ANTAGONISTIC, VIEWS OF SCRIPTURE

THE TOP 5 WORDS NON-CHRISTIAN MILLENNIALS CHOOSE TO DESCRIBE THE BIBLE

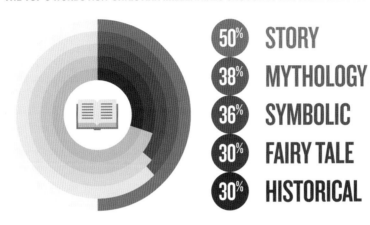

- 50% STORY
- 38% MYTHOLOGY
- 36% SYMBOLIC
- 30% FAIRY TALE
- 30% HISTORICAL

~6 **IN 10**

THE NUMBER OF NON-CHRISTIAN MILLENNIALS WHO HAVE NEVER READ THE BIBLE (62%)

WHEN THEY SEE SOMEONE READING THE BIBLE IN PUBLIC, THEY ARE MOST LIKELY TO

22%

ASSUME THE PERSON IS POLITICALLY CONSERVATIVE

21%

FIGURE THEY DON'T HAVE ANYTHING IN COMMON WITH THE PERSON

17%

THINK THE PERSON IS OLD-FASHIONED

PRACTICAL / DANGEROUS / IRRELEVANT

THE TOP 3 WAYS NON-CHRISTIANS PERCEIVE THE BIBLE

 30% THE BIBLE IS A USEFUL BOOK OF MORAL TEACHINGS

 27% THE BIBLE IS A DANGEROUS BOOK OF RELIGIOUS DOGMA USED FOR CENTURIES TO OPPRESS PEOPLE

 19% THE BIBLE IS AN OUTDATED BOOK WITH NO RELEVANCE FOR TODAY

FROM GENERATION TO GENERATION

Against national trends, practicing Protestants of all ages hold the Bible in high regard and devote significant time to its study.

The average time spent reading is 20 minutes for teens and 30 minutes for adults, including Millennials.

Together, practicing Protestants read the Bible more than 2 million hours each year.

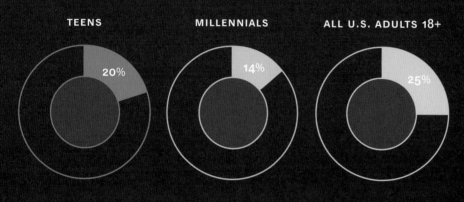

TEENS 20% **MILLENNIALS** 14% **ALL U.S. ADULTS 18+** 25%

. . . *are practicing Protestants*

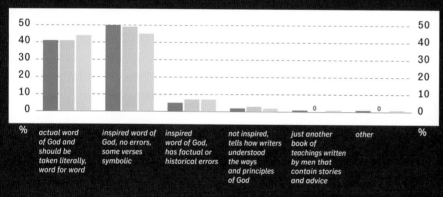

| % | actual word of God and should be taken literally, word for word | inspired word of God, no errors, some verses symbolic | inspired word of God, has factual or historical errors | not inspired, tells how writers understood the ways and principles of God | just another book of teachings written by men that contain stories and advice | other | % |

Among practicing Protestants, nine out of 10 in every age group say either that the Bible is the actual word of God or that it's the inspired word of God without error.

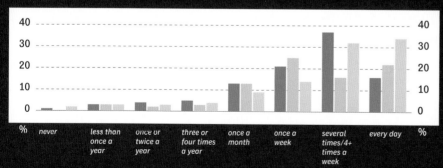

| % | never | less than once a year | once or twice a year | three or four times a year | once a month | once a week | several times/4+ times a week | every day | % |

Bible readership is robust among these practicing Christians. Two-thirds or more read the Scriptures at least once a week, and over one-third read four or more times per week.

Barna / American Bible Society 2015–2016; n=1,056 teens; n=2,008 adults. Totals may not equal 100 percent due to rounding.

14 WHAT YOUNGER GENERATIONS BELIEVE

Young adults and teens, as a group, share a fairly "high" view of the Scriptures and tend to hold the Bible in high regard—not just as a historical document or set of useful teachings, but as a divinely inspired book. Two out of three Millennials (61%) and seven in 10 teens (70%) hold one of the three views of the Bible that fall within historic Christian orthodoxy, with a plurality in each group believing "the Bible is the inspired word of God and has no errors, although some verses are meant to be symbolic rather than literal" (34%).

However, roughly one in five teens and one in three Millennials believe the Bible is *not* divinely inspired. Eleven percent of Millennials and 8 percent of teens say "the Bible was not inspired by God but tells how the writers of the Bible understood the ways and principles of God," and an additional one in four Millennials (23%) and one in seven teens (14%) take the "lowest" view: "The Bible is just another book of teachings written by men that contains stories and advice."

These beliefs come into stark relief when seen through the lens of generation. Overall Millennials and teens continue, along with older Americans, to see the Bible as sacred—but they are less likely to do so than older generations. The contrast is most obvious between Millennials and Elders: Young adults are twice as likely as Elders to say the Bible is "just another book of teachings written by men" (23% vs. 11%) and half as likely to believe it is the actual word of God (16% vs. 31%). But Millennials' younger counterparts, teens 13 to 17, are more similar in belief to their Gen-X parents—which makes sense, as teens living at home tend to be under greater parental influence than young adults out on their own.[5]

2 OUT OF 3 MILLENNIALS AND 7 OUT OF 10 TEENS HOLD AN ORTHODOX VIEW OF THE BIBLE

THE BEST DEFINITION OF THE BIBLE

% among U.S. teens and adults 13 and older

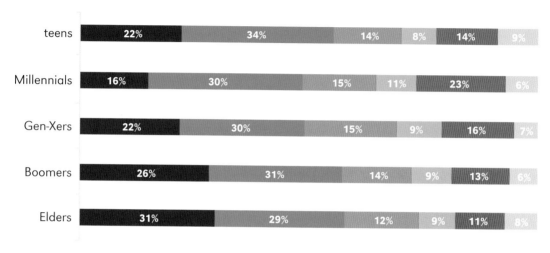

teens	22%	34%	14%	8%	14%	9%
Millennials	16%	30%	15%	11%	23%	6%
Gen-Xers	22%	30%	15%	9%	16%	7%
Boomers	26%	31%	14%	9%	13%	6%
Elders	31%	29%	12%	9%	11%	8%

a. **The actual word of God** and should be taken literally, word for word

b. **The inspired word of God** and has no errors, although some verses are meant to be symbolic rather than literal

c. **The inspired word of God** but has some factual or historical errors

d. Not inspired by God but tells how the writers of the Bible understood the ways and principles of God

e. Just another book of teaching written by men that contains stories and advice

f. Other / don't know

Skepticism about the Bible is more common among younger Americans than among Boomers and Elders. Yet once again there are bright, countercultural trends among practicing Christians, and remarkable consistency across age groups. The share of

THE BEST DEFINITION OF THE BIBLE: PRACTICING CHRISTIANS

% among U.S. practicing Christian teens and adults 13 and older

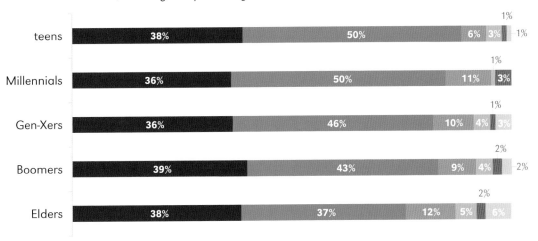

teens	38%	50%	6%	3%	1% / 1%
Millennials	36%	50%	11%	3%	1%
Gen-Xers	36%	46%	10%	4%	3% / 1%
Boomers	39%	43%	9%	4%	2% / 2%
Elders	38%	37%	12%	5%	6% / 2%

practicing Christians among teens (30%) and Millennials (19%) are a smaller proportion than among older generations (29% Gen-Xers, 36% Boomers, 45% Elders), but their beliefs about the Bible are quite similar to older practicing Christians'.

In a 2014 nationwide study of Millennials, Barna asked participants to identify which statement comes closest to their personal beliefs about the Bible. A plurality of all Millennials (30%), including non-Christians, says it is a useful book of moral teachings. Practicing Christian Millennials are most likely to say it is "the inspired word of God" (22%), followed by a tie between "a useful book of moral teachings" (21%) and "the inerrant, infallible, living word of God" (21%). A startling 27 percent of non-Christian Millennials would go so far as to say they believe the Bible is "a dangerous book of religious dogma used for centuries to oppress people." But one in five takes a slightly less antagonistic approach, dismissing the Bible as simply "an outdated book with no relevance for today" (19%).

MILLENNIALS' DESCRIPTIONS OF THE BIBLE

The following are different statements about the Bible. Which comes closest to describing what you believe about the Bible?

	% ALL MILLENNIALS	% PRACTICING CHRISTIANS	% NON-PRACTICING CHRISTIANS	% NON-CHRISTIANS
The Bible is a useful book of moral teachings	30	21	35	30
The Bible is the inspired word of God	15	22	18	8
The Bible is a dangerous book of religious dogma used for centuries to oppress people	13	9	4	27
The Bible, though flawed, points to God and his teachings for us	12	5	18	9
The Bible is inspiring and should be read by everyone	11	17	14	5
The Bible is an outdated book with no relevance for today	10	6	6	19
The Bible is the inerrant, infallible, living word of God	8	21	6	4

The Bible as a Guide for Life

In the same survey, Millennials were asked where they learned or discovered absolute moral truth. Nearly four in 10 practicing Christian Millennials (39%) say the Bible is their main source of moral truth, followed by the church (16%) and their parents (14%). For non-Christians, parents serve as the main source of moral truth (28%), followed by their feelings (16%) and experiences (13%). Only 7 percent of non-Christians say the Bible serves as a main source of moral truth in their life.

MILLENNIALS' SOURCES OF MORAL TRUTH

What is the main source from which you have learned or discovered absolute moral truths and standards?

% among those who believe moral truth is absolute

	% ALL MILLENNIALS	% PRACTICING CHRISTIANS	% NON-PRACTICING CHRISTIANS	% NON-CHRISTIANS
Bible	26	39	23	7
parents: views / values they taught you	19	14	19	28
church	15	16	19	7
experiences you've had	9	8	7	13
feelings	8	4	9	16
friends: conversations, behavior	6	5	5	9
God speaking directly to you	6	4	7	5
society: preferences, traditions, norms	5	4	4	8
Golden Rule	3	1	5	3
media: TV, movies, publications	2	3	1	2
laws and public policies	*	1	0	0
other	1	0	1	2

*Indicates less than one-half of one percent

In the general U.S. population, younger generations are less convinced than older adults about the Bible's sufficiency as a guide to a life of meaning. About one-third of Millennials (32%)

says the Bible contains everything one needs to know to live a meaningful life, compared to two out of three Elders (61%) and more than half of Boomers (55%). This is an enormous disparity and, unless there is a dramatic shift among Millennials, their perceptions point to what will eventually become the majority view.

Among practicing Christians, on the other hand, generational differences on this question are significantly slimmer. Practicing Christian Millennials, who say their faith is very important and attend church at least once a month, are much more like their older sisters and brothers in the faith than like their generational counterparts outside the Church. In every age group, practicing Christians are strongly convinced of the Bible's sufficiency.

THE BIBLE CONTAINS EVERYTHING A PERSON NEEDS TO KNOW TO LIVE A MEANINGFUL LIFE

% agree strongly among U.S. teens and adults 13 and older

● all U.S.   ● practicing Christians

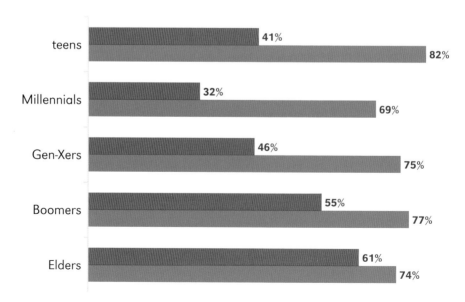

teens — 41% / 82%

Millennials — 32% / 69%

Gen-Xers — 46% / 75%

Boomers — 55% / 77%

Elders — 61% / 74%

Teens & the Bible

Teens read the Bible less frequently than older adults—but some teens read more frequently than others. Six out of 10 African American teens (59%) are Bible readers (that is, they read the Bible at least three or four times a year), compared to half of Hispanic youth (51%) and only four in 10 white teens (42%). Three-quarters of black teens also say the Bible has a lot (44%) or some (30%) influence on their lives, compared to two-thirds of Hispanics (64%) and fewer than six in 10 whites (57%).

As one might expect, when it comes to the Bible's influence, practicing Protestants (98%) and Catholics (97%) are far more likely than their peers who are non-practicing Christians (55%) or of another or no faith (26%) to say the Scriptures have at least some influence on their lives.

But that doesn't mean they always feel good when they read it.

What They Feel

In the 2015 "State of the Bible: Teens" study commissioned by American Bible Society, Barna discovered significant differences between how teens and adults feel after reading the Bible. Researchers asked survey participants who had ever read or heard the Bible read aloud to identify the primary emotion they experienced the last time they engaged with the Scriptures. By and large, teens are less likely than both Millennials and U.S. adults overall to report positive emotions and more likely to report negative feelings. In fact, only one in six teens (18%) reports no unfavorable emotions, compared to more than half of all adults (54%). Instead, teens say they felt confused (28%), overwhelmed (19%) or bored (19%).

TEENS ARE MORE LIKELY THAN BOTH MILLENNIALS AND U.S. ADULTS OVERALL TO REPORT NEGATIVE EMOTIONS AFTER READING THE BIBLE

TEENS' FAVORABLE EMOTIONS

The last time you read or heard the Bible, what was the primary favorable emotion you experienced, if any? (multiple response)

	% TEENS	% MILLENNIALS	% ALL ADULTS
peaceful	28	31	43
encouraged / inspired	22	35	38
a sense of direction	21	30	31
hopeful	15	26	34
happy	11	23	26

TEENS' UNFAVORABLE EMOTIONS

The last time you read or heard the Bible, what was the primary unfavorable emotion you experienced, if any? (multiple response)

	% TEENS	% MILLENNIALS	% ALL ADULTS
confused	28	19	14
overwhelmed	19	15	13
bored	19	13	6
doubtful	6	13	9
discouraged	4	7	6
convicted, guilty, sinful	2	*	1

*Indicates less than one-half of one percent

Teens who practice Christianity report more favorable emotions than their peers after having read the Bible—but, in some cases, more unfavorable emotions, too. Practicing Protestants are more likely than average to report feeling encouraged or inspired (30% vs. 22% among all teens) and practicing Catholics are more likely to say they felt peaceful (42% vs. 28%). However, more Catholics (39%) than teens overall (28%) report feeling confused, and more Protestants say they felt overwhelmed after reading or hearing the Bible. These mixed emotions indicate an area of need and a window of opportunity for leaders who can help teenagers interpret the Scriptures and apply what they understand to their lives and relationships.

Barna also asked teens to identify the woman who has a book in the Bible named after her and they are nearly as likely as adults to choose the correct answer, Esther (52% vs. 57%), and more likely than Millennials (41%) to do so. Six in 10 teens (61%) are also able to identify Isaac as Abraham's son, which is on par with U.S. adults (59%) and better than Millennials (54%). All in

TEENS' MIXED EMOTIONS INDICATE AN OPPORTUNITY FOR LEADERS WHO CAN HELP THEM INTERPRET AND APPLY THE SCRIPTURES

BIBLICAL LITERACY AMONG TEENS

Which of the following statements is found in the Bible?

	% TEENS	% MILLENNIALS	% ALL ADULTS
God works in mysterious ways	25	30	36
The truth will set you free	22	25	24
To thine own self be true	18	23	17
God helps those who help themselves	14	15	13
none of these / not sure	22	8	10

IF TEENS FOLLOW IN
THE FOOTSTEPS OF
OLDER MILLENNIALS,
A SIGNIFICANT NUMBER
WILL DROP OUT OF
CHURCH INVOLVEMENT
DURING THEIR
TWENTIES

all, teens prove to be at least as Bible literate as many adults and often more literate than twentysomethings.

Teens' comparative familiarity with the Scriptures is likely due to the fact that a higher proportion of them (26%) compared with Millennials (19%) are practicing Christians who continue to regularly attend church. If they follow in the footsteps of older Millennials, however, a significant number will drop out of church involvement, at least for a time, during their 20s. (Barna asked teens if they plan to attend a church after high school: 70 percent of practicing Protestants and 56 percent of practicing Catholics say it is "very likely.")

But their current connections to a faith community represent a window of opportunity for deepening Bible engagement—and Part V explores some ideas for how to make the most of the opportunities.

15 HOW YOUNGER GENERATIONS ENGAGE

Millennials and teens read the Bible less frequently than older adults, but practicing Christian Millennials are again more similar to older Christians than they are to their age cohort more generally. Practicing Christian teens read the Bible less frequently than older practicing Christians, but more often than their age group in the general population: One-third reads at least once a week, compared to only one-quarter of all U.S. teens.

HOW FREQUENTLY PEOPLE READ THE BIBLE: PRACTICING CHRISTIANS VS. ALL AMERICANS

% among U.S. teens and adults 13 and older

● every day   ● once / week   ● 3-4 times / year   ● < once / year
● several times / week   ● once / month   ● 1-2 times / year   ● never

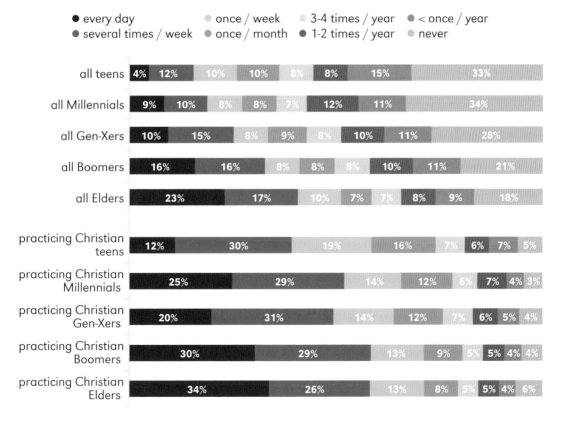

	every day	several times / week	once / week	once / month	3-4 times / year	1-2 times / year	< once / year	never
all teens	4%	12%	10%	10%	8%	8%	15%	33%
all Millennials	9%	10%	8%	8%	7%	12%	11%	34%
all Gen-Xers	10%	15%	8%	9%	8%	10%	11%	28%
all Boomers	16%	16%	8%	8%	8%	10%	11%	21%
all Elders	23%	17%	10%	7%	7%	8%	9%	18%
practicing Christian teens	12%	30%	19%	16%	7%	6%	7%	5%
practicing Christian Millennials	25%	29%	14%	12%	6%	7%	4%	3%
practicing Christian Gen-Xers	20%	31%	14%	12%	7%	6%	5%	4%
practicing Christian Boomers	30%	29%	13%	9%	5%	5%	4%	4%
practicing Christian Elders	34%	26%	13%	8%	5%	5%	4%	6%

How Millennials Read the Bible

Bible reading among Millennials is primarily a solitary activity; the majority says they most often read the Bible on their own. This is even truer for practicing Christians, nearly two-thirds of whom say they most often read the Bible "by myself." When they do read it with other people, it is generally at church: Half of practicing Christian Millennials say they are most likely to engage with the Bible by hearing it read aloud at church.

HOW MILLENNIALS ENGAGE WITH THE BIBLE

Thinking about your Bible reading in the past month, how did you usually engage with the Bible?

	% ALL MILLENNIALS	% PRACTICING CHRISTIANS	% NON-PRACTICING CHRISTIANS	% NON-CHRISTIANS
Read it by myself	54	64	47	35
Heard it read aloud in church	41	50	34	26
Prayed about what I read	33	39	24	35
Discussed it with friends or family	31	40	21	29
Read it with a devotional	29	35	21	32
Made notes or underlined verses	28	35	19	30
Read it as part of a one-year plan to read the full Bible	27	34	21	18
Read it in conjunction with a liturgy or prayer	27	29	23	30
Memorized scripture	26	30	21	22
Read it with a commentary or Bible resource	24	27	18	27
With a small group	21	28	13	21

HOW MILLENNIALS APPROACH THE BIBLE

When you read the Bible, how often do you use the following approaches?

% "often" among those who have ever read the Bible

	% ALL MILLENNIALS	% PRACTICING CHRISTIANS	% NON-PRACTICING CHRISTIANS	% NON-CHRISTIANS
In search of a specific verse or verses	32	40	29	26
As you feel led by the Spirit	30	48	23	17
One book at a time	29	39	23	25
From front to back	28	41	20	26
With a devotional	22	35	16	16
Chronologically	21	36	12	19
As part of a guided plan (like a one-year plan)	21	33	16	11

Millennials engage with the Bible in a number of ways while they read— from praying regularly about what they're reading, to reading along with a devotional, to making notes and underlining verses. Practicing Christian Millennials, in particular, make use of a number of reading methods and resources. Common practices include reading it as part of a one-year plan to read the entire Bible, reading it in conjunction with a liturgy or prayer and memorizing Scripture (and reading it with a commentary or Bible resource.

When they do sit down to read, how do Millennials approach the text? And what do they read most often? Practicing Christian Millennials say they are most likely to approach reading the Bible as they feel led by the Spirit (48%), followed by from front to back (41%) and in search of a specific verse or verses (40%). Other common approaches include reading one book at a time (39%), with a devotional (35%), chronologically (36%) and as part of a guided plan (such as a one-year plan, 33%).

Those who engage with the Bible less often—specifically, non-practicing Christian Millennials—are most likely, when they do read the Bible, to pick it up in search of a specific verse or verses (29%). They also read as they feel led by the Spirit (23%) or one book at a time (23%). They are less likely to read from front to back (20%), with a devotional (16%), chronologically (12%) or as part of a guided plan (16%).

Why Millennials Read (and Don't Read) the Bible

For Millennials who do read the Bible, what motivates them to read? Most Bible readers (who read at least three to four times a year) in every generation say they read because doing so brings them closer to God. However, Millennials (21%) are more likely than both younger (6%) and older Bible readers (15%) to say their main motivation is they have a problem to solve or they need direction. This represents an important window of opportunity for ministry, as Randy Petersen explores in a special report, "When Life Stops Making Sense," on page 63.

Like most Americans, young adults and teens wish they read the Bible more often. More than half (56% of Millennials and 62% of teens) say so, compared to 62 percent of all adults. The desire appears to be most prevalent among practicing and non-practicing Christians, though even a significant number of non-Christians—whom one might assume have little motivation to pick up a Bible—desire to read it more often than they do.

While most Millennials desire to read the Bible more, they are more likely than older adults to say their Bible reading decreased over the past year. It's unclear why this is the case among teens, but because Millennials are the adult generation most likely to

DESIRE TO READ THE BIBLE

Do you wish that you read the Bible more, or not?

	% TEENS	% ALL MILLENNIALS	% PRACTICING CHRISTIANS	% NON-PRACTICING CHRISTIANS	% NON-CHRISTIANS
yes	62	56	92	65	17
no	38	43	5	19	71
don't know	0	1	2	16	12

REASONS PEOPLE READ THE BIBLE

The following are some reasons a person might read the Bible. Which statement is most true for you?

	% TEENS	% MILLENNIALS 18–31	% GEN-XERS 32–50	% BOOMERS 51–69	% ELDERS 70+
It brings me closer to God	60	50	57	60	61
I know I'm supposed to	15	5	5	4	4
I need comfort	8	12	13	14	15
I have a problem I need to solve or I need direction	6	21	18	16	11
It is part of my studies at school	4	7	2	2	3
not sure / some other reason	8	5	4	5	6

drop out of church involvement, this also makes them more likely to push pause on spiritual disciplines like Bible reading. As we saw in Part II, about one in six adults who reports less frequent Bible reading (17%) attributes the decrease to their disconnection from a church community.

Among Millennials who reported an increase in Bible reading in the 2014 study, the most common cause for the increase was an understanding that Bible reading is an important part of their faith journey (41%). Other significant contributors included seeing how the Bible changed someone they know for the better (31%), a significant life change (29%), downloading the Bible onto a smartphone or tablet (29%), going to a church where the Bible became more accessible (28%), having a conversation with a Christian friend (27%), following media conversations about religion and spirituality (26%), watching *The Bible* miniseries on television (24%), joining a group that uses the Bible (22%) and having someone they know ask them to read the Bible together (19%). The number who selected each of these as contributing factors to their increase in Bible engagement is striking: Even the lowest-rated reason—having a friend ask

TEENS AND MILLENNIALS ARE MORE LIKELY THAN OTHER ADULTS TO SAY THEIR BIBLE READING DECREASED OVER THE PAST YEAR

BIBLE USE INCREASED, DECREASED OR STAYED THE SAME

Would you say that your own personal use of the Bible has increased, decreased or is about the same as one year ago?

	% TEENS	% ALL MILLENNIALS	% PRACTICING CHRISTIANS	% NON-PRACTICING CHRISTIANS	% NON-CHRISTIANS
stayed the same	71	64	66	67	67
gone up	17	20	24	24	24
gone down	12	11	7	6	7

REASONS FOR INCREASED BIBLE ENGAGEMENT

What do you think caused the increase in your
Bible engagement? (multiple response)

	% ALL MILLENNIALS	% NON-PRACTICING CHRISTIANS	% NON-CHRISTIANS
I came to understand it as an important part of my faith journey	41	44	36
I saw how the Bible changed someone I know for the better	31	34	28
I had a significant change in my life (marriage, birth of a child, etc.)	29	30	31
I downloaded the Bible onto my smartphone or tablet	29	28	32
I went to a church where the Bible became more accessible to me	28	35	21
A difficult experience in my life caused me to search the Bible for direction and answers	28	28	30
I had a conversation with a Christian friend	27	26	25

them to read the Bible together—was chosen by nearly one in five Millennials who upped their engagement.

Among Millennials who reported a decrease in Bible engagement, the main culprit is simply lack of time. A plurality of all Millennials (39%) and a majority of non-practicing Christian Millennials (49%) say the main reason they haven't read the Bible as much is because they got too busy with life's responsibilities. This is less of a factor for non-Christians, who stopped reading simply because they stopped believing: Nearly half say the reason they decreased their Bible engagement is because they became atheist or agnostic (46%), while another 20 percent say they decided to leave church altogether.

REASONS FOR DECREASED BIBLE ENGAGEMENT

What do you think caused the decrease in your
Bible engagement? (multiple response)

	% ALL MILLENNIALS	% NON-PRACTICING CHRISTIANS	% NON-CHRISTIANS
I got too busy with life's responsibilities (job, family, etc.)	39	49	18
I became atheist or agnostic	21	6	46
I had a significant change in my life (loss of a job, death of a loved one, etc.)	18	21	10
A difficult experience in my life caused me to doubt my faith (or God and the Bible)	13	13	13
I decided to leave the church altogether	13	9	20
I saw how reading the Bible made very little difference in the life of someone I know	9	8	11
I converted to another faith	8	4	13
I followed media discussions around religion and spirituality	8	8	10
I had conversation with a non-Christian friend	7	9	4

*Practicing Christians not included due to small sample size.

Another factor for non-practicing Christians is a negative life experience, such as losing a job, the death of a loved one, etc. Presumably for this group, the negative experience shifted their views or priorities. About 13 percent say so explicitly—that "a difficult experience in life caused me to doubt my faith."

Aside from not having enough time to read the Bible (19% of all Millennials, 33% of practicing Christians, 22% of non-practicing Christians), what other frustrations do Millennials feel

FRUSTRATIONS WITH BIBLE READING

Which of the following would you say is your most significant frustration when it comes to reading the Bible?

	% ALL MILLENNIALS	% PRACTICING CHRISTIANS	% NON-PRACTICING CHRISTIANS	% NON-CHRISTIANS
You never seem to have enough time to read it	19	33	22	7
You do not read the Bible	19	1	10	42
You find the language difficult to relate to	13	13	17	8
You don't feel that excited about reading it	15	9	19	15
You don't understand the background or the history of the Bible	9	13	11	5
You can never find the stories or verses you are looking for	4	6	3	3

toward Bible reading? For non-practicing Christians, it is often a lack of desire: about one-fifth say they just don't feel that excited about reading it (19%). They also find the language difficult to relate to (17%) and don't always understand the background or history of the Bible (11%).

For practicing Christians, they most often feel the latter two frustrations: They don't understand the background or history of the Bible (13%) or they find the language difficult to relate to (13%). For non-Christians (aside from just not reading the Bible, 42%), their primary frustration is that they don't feel excited about reading it (15%).

When they have trouble understanding the Bible, or come across a passage they don't agree with, where do Millennials go for guidance?

RESOURCES FOR UNDERSTANDING THE BIBLE

What do you do when you read something in the Bible that you don't understand or don't agree with? (multiple response)

	% ALL MILLENNIALS	% PRACTICING CHRISTIANS	% NON-PRACTICING CHRISTIANS	% NON-CHRISTIANS
I do research in commentaries or study guides	32	40	27	30
I pray about it	31	44	27	19
I ask a pastor or church leader	28	45	21	16
I go online to read what other people think about those passages	24	25	24	21
I ignore it or move on	20	13	20	34
I don't feel like I have to believe every part of the Bible	19	8	22	30
I don't have to understand everything, so I accept it as true	16	17	16	13
It makes me doubt God	10	12	8	11

Practicing Christians are most likely to go to a pastor or church leader for help (45%). They also pray about it (44%) or do some research on the passage in commentaries or study guides (40%). A smaller number go online to read what other people think about those passages (25%).

Non-practicing Christians are most apt either to research the passage in commentaries or study guides (27%) or to pray about the verses (27%). About one-quarter (24%) goes online to see what others think and one-fifth asks a pastor or church leader. Non-practicing Christians are much more likely than practicing Christians to say they don't feel like they have to believe every part of the Bible (22% vs. 8%), and very few say the troubling verses make them doubt God (8%).

Among non-Christians, the most common response to a problematic passage in the Bible is to ignore it and move on (34%).

Engagement Across Generations

A combination of beliefs and reading frequency leads us, of course, to Bible engagement. As we found in Part 1, Bible engagement in the general population contracts with each successively younger generation. In 2016, Millennials (11%) are half as likely as Elders (25%) to be Bible engaged and twice as likely to be Bible skeptics (26% vs. 13%). And because of their low reading frequency, teens are even less likely to be Bible engaged (7%).

Yet Bible engagement is strong across all age demographics of practicing Christians—with the exception of practicing Christian teens who, while surpassing their peers overall, are less likely to be Bible engaged compared to older practicing Christians, thanks to their lower reading frequency.

BIBLE ENGAGEMENT IS STRONG ACROSS ALL AGE DEMOGRAPHICS OF PRACTICING CHRISTIANS

BIBLE ENGAGEMENT IN AMERICA 2016:
PRACTICING CHRISTIANS VS. ALL U.S. ADULTS & TEENS

% among U.S. teens and adults 13 and older

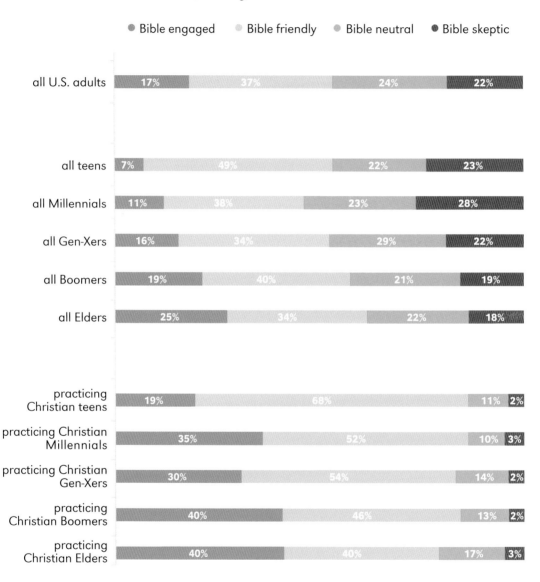

● Bible engaged   ● Bible friendly   ● Bible neutral   ● Bible skeptic

	Bible engaged	Bible friendly	Bible neutral	Bible skeptic
all U.S. adults	17%	37%	24%	22%
all teens	7%	49%	22%	23%
all Millennials	11%	38%	23%	28%
all Gen-Xers	16%	34%	29%	22%
all Boomers	19%	40%	21%	19%
all Elders	25%	34%	22%	18%
practicing Christian teens	19%	68%	11%	2%
practicing Christian Millennials	35%	52%	10%	3%
practicing Christian Gen-Xers	30%	54%	14%	2%
practicing Christian Boomers	40%	46%	13%	2%
practicing Christian Elders	40%	40%	17%	3%

Q&A WITH **REV. ROB HOSKINS**

Q: OneHope's landmark Attitudes and Behaviors of Youth (ABY) research among teens 13 to 19 in 44 countries found that a high level of Bible engagement is a strong predictor of positive teen behaviors. This is great news! Why do you think Bible reading and behaviors are so strongly correlated?

REV. ROB HOSKINS

Rob Hoskins was born to missionary parents, which is where his passion to spread the truth in God's word began. He has served with OneHope for more than 26 years, and has been president since 2004. Rob is an ordained general-appointed missionary of the Assemblies of God and currently serves as Chair of the Board of Trustees at Oral Roberts University.

A: In an increasingly relativistic and pluralistic world, where foundational truths are undermined, many young people struggle with insecurity, indecision and even fear. Having the Bible as an authoritative text and engaging with it consistently provide the confidence, security and certitude that many youth lack today.

God's word is powerful, and it changes lives. We know that the message of Christ's love and redemption speaks not only to a teenager's eternity but also to his or her present reality. Our ABY research reveals the three major factors that influence young people; one of them is engagement with religious texts. When teens read the Bible—more so than any other religious text—they build the strongest foundation to stand strong against negative cultural influences, and instead make positive life choices. For instance, teens who read the Bible at least monthly:

- Have better relationships with parents and purpose for living
- Engage in significantly less sexual activity, substance use, crime, lying and physical aggression
- Are nine times more likely to believe the Bible provides a clear and indisputable description of moral truth
- Are 10 times more likely to find their faith is important to them
- Are nearly four times more likely to believe that prayer can change what happens in life
- Are more than five times more likely to recall a time when their religious beliefs changed the way they behaved

Q: OneHope puts great emphasis on developing digital tools to help kids engage with the Scriptures. How have you seen these tools increase or deepen Bible engagement?

A: The potential in the digital space is unlimited! It has been exciting to see some innovative approaches—like augmented reality, social media platforms and "gameification"—connect with 21st-century digital natives. Not only are they increasing biblical literacy, but also repetitive engagement with God's word is developing their spiritual formation as truth from the Bible is cemented deeply into their hearts. The practical applications give young people an outlet for not only taking in God's word, but also sharing it with others with a single tap or click. We are hearing stories of children bringing parents and grandparents to Christ by insisting they "play the Bible" together or by watching the testimony they created and shared on social media. And some digital programs are being used in ways we never imagined—ESL programs, for example. People trying to learn English are practicing by reading stories from the Bible, and then coming to faith! We are also excited about resourcing churches with tools that give youth leaders and parents the ability to track their children's Bible reading and comprehension, and their practice of spiritual disciplines like prayer, giving and service projects.

Q: What excites you most about the next 10 years? Where do you see the most fertile ground for God's word to take root and bear fruit?

A: I'm so excited about new frontiers for sharing God's word. The potential of digital is immense—we're living a "Gutenberg moment," where technology is allowing us to take the Scriptures farther, faster and into places where the printed Bible cannot go. For instance, the Bible App for Kids has been downloaded in *every* country in the world, even ones where the Bible is banned!

Another frontier ripe for harvest is unreached people groups. There are new methods speeding up the Bible translation process that not only get the Scriptures into new languages, but that also utilize highly innovative and relevant delivery methods. We are seeing unrivaled success with contextualized programs in some of the most fertile ground in the world: the Sahel region of Africa, which is predominantly Muslim.

Everywhere seed is being thrown, it's taking root and growing quickly. People are hungry for the hope and freedom that can be found in Christ. Every week we have reports of hundreds of new believers. We can hardly plant churches fast enough for the number of new believers. God's word is truly going forth like never before!

16 MILLENNIALS & THE BIBLE "BRAND"

As Barna explored at length in *Making Space for Millennials*,[6] the generation as a whole tends to be hyperaware of marketing messages, images and branding—which caused us to wonder, *How do young adults view the "brand" of the Bible?* In the 2014 national study of young adults commissioned by American Bible Society, researchers found significant differences, when it comes to the Bible's brand, between practicing Christians, non-practicing Christians and non-Christians.

Word Associations

Presented with a list of words to describe the Bible, choices vary according to Millennials' beliefs and practices. Practicing Christians' top five choices reflect a belief in the Scriptures' veracity and divine origins: *fact* (63%), *testimony* (53%), *sacred* (52%), *historical* (47%) and *revelation* (46%). Non-practicing Christian Millennials are more likely to choose words that treat the Bible more as an artifact, a witness to a religious tradition and its beliefs: *historical* (47%), *symbolic* (42%), *sacred* (38%), *testimony* (37%) and *story* (33%). And non-Christian Millennials prefer words that place the Bible within the realm of other religious books or cultural legends, such as *story* (50%), *mythology* (38%), *symbolic* (36%), *historical* (30%) and even *fairy tale* (30%).

Brand Messages

When asked to choose what they believe are the top two or three main messages of the Bible, a plurality of Millennials point to "There is only one God" as the top contender (39%). Their second choice is the Golden Rule, "Do unto others as you would have them do unto you" (35%). And rounding out the top three is a narrative storyline, that "humans are sinful and require forgiveness

WHEN IT COMES TO THE BIBLE'S BRAND, THERE ARE SIGNIFICANT DIFFERENCES BETWEEN PRACTICING CHRISTIANS, NON-PRACTICING CHRISTIANS AND NON-CHRISTIAN MILLENNIALS

BEST DESCRIPTIONS OF THE BIBLE

Which words best reflect your beliefs about the Christian Bible? (multiple response)

	% ALL MILLENNIALS	% PRACTICING CHRISTIANS	% NON-PRACTICING CHRISTIANS	% NON-CHRISTIANS
historical	41	47	47	30
symbolic	38	35	42	36
story	38	31	33	50
sacred	32	52	38	12
testimony	31	53	37	11
fact	29	63	27	10
book of rules	28	36	31	20
revelation	26	46	29	8
mythology	22	14	14	38
fairy tale	15	7	7	30
authoritative	14	27	12	8
dogmatic	10	11	8	11
propaganda	10	8	4	19
manifesto	9	14	9	5
infallible	8	20	5	3
inerrant	6	14	5	2

and redemption" (32%). As on other questions, non-practicing Christians reflect the choices of the generation overall, though they slightly prefer the Golden Rule (42%) over the message of one God (38%). Non-Christian Millennials' top three answers are the same as non-practicing Christians', but in a different order of preference. They point to the Golden Rule as the Bible's primary message (36%), followed by the narrative of redemption, "Humans are sinful and require forgiveness and redemption" (35%) and the statement "There is only one God" (32%).

MAIN MESSAGES OF THE BIBLE

What would you say are the two or three main messages of the Bible? (multiple response)

	% ALL MILLENNIALS	% PRACTICING CHRISTIANS	% NON-PRACTICING CHRISTIANS	% NON-CHRISTIANS
There is only one God	39	53	38	32
Do unto others as you would have them do unto you	35	18	42	36
Humans are sinful and require forgiveness and redemption	32	29	32	35
Jesus is the only way to eternal life	28	46	26	19
God helps those who help themselves	25	24	26	23
You can discover freedom, hope and joy	24	27	26	18
Humans need God	23	31	22	18
This is how you can live well and obey God	21	22	21	20
Here is the way to get to heaven	17	21	14	17

Such similarities between non-practicing Christians and non-Christians indicate that these are the primary messages "outsiders" hear about the Bible from culture or from Christians and the Church. It is encouraging that such positive themes—and, indeed, a gospel summary—continue to be absorbed by the broader culture.

Today's Market

Beyond its sweeping themes, what does the Bible have to say about the pressing issues of our day? Most Millennials agree the Bible encourages some positive human behaviors—among them, forgiveness (78%), patience (76%) and generosity (75%)—and discourages some negative human activities—for example, war (49%), slavery (46%), prostitution (61%), gambling (59%) and pornography (56%).

There are a few issues, however, on which Christian and non-Christian readings of the Bible diverge. On the question of social justice, seven in 10 practicing Christians are convinced the Bible encourages it (69%), while non-Christians are less persuaded: Only 41 percent say the Bible encourages social justice; 17 percent say it discourages it; 18 percent think the Bible is silent on the topic; and one-quarter isn't sure what the Bible has to say about social justice.

CHRISTIAN AND NON-CHRISTIAN MILLENNIALS ARE NOT ON THE SAME PAGE WHEN IT COMES TO WHAT THE BIBLE SAYS ABOUT SAME-SEX RELATIONSHIPS

Similarly, Christian and non-Christian Millennials are not on the same page when it comes to what the Bible says about one of society's most contested issues: same-sex relationships. Practicing Christians (1%) are less likely than non-Christians (5%) to say the Bible encourages same-sex relationships; more likely to say it discourages them (87% vs. 57% of non-Christians); and three times less likely to say the Bible is silent on the issue (12% vs. 38%).

The Bible in Public

In the 2014 study of Millennials and the 2015 study of teens, Barna asked what young people think when they see someone reading the Scriptures in public. Among the wider U.S. population, teens and young adults express mildly positive or neutral feelings, while

PERCEPTIONS OF THOSE WHO READ THE BIBLE IN PUBLIC

What do you think when you see someone else reading the Bible in a public place?

	% TEENS	% PRACTICING CHRISTIAN TEENS	% MILLENNIALS	% PRACTICING CHRISTIAN MILLENNIALS
I am happy to see other Christians around	39	75	29	57
I feel grateful to see that sacred books are still important to people	39	59	26	44
I feel joyful	31	63	27	56
I feel encouraged	28	63	29	57
It reminds me to read my own Bible	28	55	24	53
I feel like they are a kindred spirit	21	41	18	34
I feel like stopping and saying hello	12	28	12	23
I think the person is old-fashioned	10	3	12	10
I feel curious about what's in the Bible	8	10	11	14
I think they should read the Bible in private	7	2	10	9
I feel uncomfortable	6	6	8	2
I assume the person is politically conservative	6	2	15	13
I suspect the person is trying to make a statement or be provocative	5	2	12	11
I figure I don't have anything in common with the person	4	0	12	8
I think the person is naïve	3	0	8	5
I feel guilty	2	2	6	10
I get embarrassed for them	1	0	6	8
none of these	23	2	19	3

practicing Christians report much more positive responses. As might be expected, a non-Christian's reaction to someone reading the Bible in public is less enthusiastic than a practicing Christian's. In fact, the primary feelings non-Christians experience are alienation and distance. Non-Christian Millennials say they assume the Bible reader is politically conservative (22%); that they don't have anything in common with the person (21%); that the person is old fashioned (17%); or that he or she is trying to make a statement or be provocative (15%). Fewer than one in 12 indicate any kind of positive response, such as encouragement (7%) or joy (7%). And only 9 percent say they feel curious about what's in the Bible when they see someone reading it—a finding that may disappoint Christians who hope reading in public could spark interest in the Bible.

It's interesting to note, however, that about one in 10 practicing Christian Millennials expresses guilt or various kinds of alienation that are more in keeping with their generational cohort than with practicing Christian teens. These mixed emotions likely point to the social cost, explored in the Introduction, that young adults face in order to remain faithful.

One common way young adults engage with the Bible in a digital age is to post scripture passages on social media platforms such as Twitter, Facebook and Instagram. Unsurprisingly, practicing Christians are the most likely to do so: A combined 81 percent have posted Bible verses online in the past year.

But what do others think when people post scripture passages? Similar to seeing people reading the Bible in public, the practice evokes primarily positive emotions among practicing Christians and ambivalent or negative emotions among non-Christians. The most common responses from Christians are to feel encouraged and inspired. Just over one-third finds it bold (in a good way). Non-practicing Christians generally have positive reactions to seeing scripture posted on social media, though they are more moderated than practicing Christian Millennials.

ONLY 9 PERCENT OF NON-CHRISTIAN MILLENNIALS SAY THEY FEEL CURIOUS ABOUT WHAT'S IN THE BIBLE WHEN THEY SEE SOMEONE READING IT

The most common response among non-Christians, however, is to say it bothers them if the verses are used naively or out of context (33%). Three in 10 find it irritating. Many assume the poster is judgmental or trying to evangelize. Of all the responses, non-Christians are least likely to feel inspired or encouraged when they see such posts. Such responses indicate that, like public Bible reading, the practice is primarily an encouragement to fellow insiders but may potentially turn off non-Christians.

PERCEPTIONS OF THOSE WHO POST SCRIPTURE ON SOCIAL MEDIA

What do you think when you see other people quote scripture in their social media or blogs?

	% ALL MILLENNIALS	% PRACTICING CHRISTIANS	% NON-PRACTICING CHRISTIANS	% NON-CHRISTIANS
I think it's okay sometimes if you are religious	29	22	28	33
It encourages me	27	56	27	7
It inspires me	27	53	29	9
It's fine when verses are used in context	27	27	30	24
It bothers me if they use verses naively or out of context	25	20	21	35
I think it's bold (in a good way)	22	35	24	11
I find it irritating	18	12	12	30
They are trying to evangelize	17	18	13	21
They are judgmental	15	10	11	24
They will push others away	13	12	10	18
I think that person is wrong	8	9	7	10
That person is strange	8	8	7	10

The Future of the Brand

Overall, practicing Christian young adults maintain a high opinion of the Scriptures' brand and message for today's culture. Non-practicing Christians are less positive, but hold mostly favorable views of the Bible.

Non-Christian Millennials, however, hold ambivalent or sometimes quite negative views of the Bible—and of those who read it. For many non-Christian Millennials, the Bible's "brand" is negative. And the depth and range of their perceptions signal difficult challenges ahead for young adults who still believe in the Bible. As Bible skepticism increases in their generation, Christian Millennials will have to face these criticisms head on and wrestle with the implications for their own beliefs.

Thankfully, when it comes to the Scriptures—more than many other areas of their faith—Millennial Christians are starting off on comparatively solid ground.

17 THE GOOD NEWS

THEIR COMMITMENT TO THE SCRIPTURES IS A REBUKE TO STEREOTYPES OF YOUNGER CHRISTIANS

Many Christians and Christian leaders are concerned about the next generation of Christians—and for good reason. There is certainly a well-documented trend of Millennials leaving church or turning away from faith. However, Barna research on the Bible gives church leaders some very good news about the Good Book: Active young Christians are holding true to historically orthodox beliefs about the Bible. In many ways, their commitment to the Scriptures is a rebuke to stereotypes of younger Christians.

Practicing Christian Millennials are the countertrend among their generation. On each of the questions studied in this chapter—in every survey Barna has done on the Bible in the past six years—practicing Christian Millennials align more closely with practicing Christians of all ages than they do with their generational peers. They affirm traditional views of the Bible as the actual or inspired word of God. They look to the Bible as their primary source for moral truth. They see it as a meaningful guide for life.

Not only are their beliefs on the Bible more closely aligned with older generations, their engagement is as well. Millennials are even more likely than Gen-Xers to read the Bible every day. They are proud to read the Bible in public and often share passages of scripture on social media.

These practices aren't always appreciated by others in their generation. Many Christians might hope that Bible-based films or sharing verses online would reach non-Christians, but the research suggests the opposite. Non-Christians tend to be more skeptical of Bible-based films and often feel turned off or alienated by seeing scripture shared via social media. On the other hand, in the rare cases when non-Christians increased their Bible reading in the past year, they often did so as a result of seeing how engagement with the Scriptures changed someone they knew. Such responses emphasize the importance of meaningful relationships and evidence of life transformation.

Practicing Christian Millennials are living against the cultural grain of their generation. Church leaders must recognize the difficulty of this posture and appreciate the pressure young adults experience as Millennials of faith. An important part of ministering to young Christians is equipping them to live their faith well within a skeptical culture—a topic we explore in depth in Part V.

PRACTICING CHRISTIAN MILLENNIALS ARE LIVING AGAINST THE CULTURAL GRAIN OF THEIR GENERATION

The Bible in a Post-Christian Context

In a multiphase research project commissioned to assess the state of Christianity and religious faith in Scotland, Barna discovered several interesting trends countering the overall move toward secularization. Scotland, like most European countries, is shifting away from its historically Christian heritage toward a post-Christian, non-religious culture. And what researchers discovered there offers insights to leaders concerned with how the U.S. Christian community can continue to flourish, and to advocate for the Bible, in a post-Christian context.

While about three in 10 U.S. adults are practicing Christians, only one in 10 Scots qualifies under Barna's definition (says his or her faith as very important and has attended a worship service in the past month). Among younger generations, the proportions are even slimmer. And yet, Scottish adults under the age of 45 (23%) are twice as likely as older adults (12%) to say "faith has transformed my life," and less likely to say faith "has not made much of a difference" (39% vs. 48%) or "has been helpful but has not greatly transformed me" (34% vs. 43%). Since it is comparatively rare for young Scots to have been raised in church, this data indicates that young adults who have a religious faith embrace it by choice rather than by inheritance or cultural default.

Interestingly, young Scots in the general population are more likely than older adults to hold an orthodox view of the Bible (that it's the actual or inspired word of God; 36% vs. 29% among all adults), even though they are less familiar with the Scriptures. They also express greater interest in finding out what wisdom the Bible might offer for their lives.

Transforming Scotland: The State of Christianity, Faith and the Church in Scotland (Barna, 2015) is a Barna report produced in partnership with Transforming Scotland and the Maclellan Foundation.

INTEREST IN LEARNING FROM THE BIBLE

% among Scottish adults 18 and older

● all adults   ● ages 18 to 24

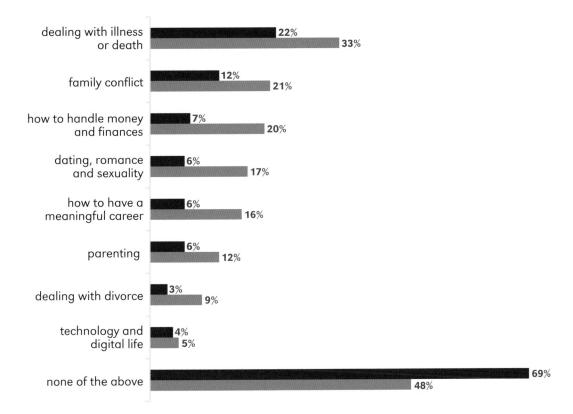

dealing with illness or death — 22% / 33%
family conflict — 12% / 21%
how to handle money and finances — 7% / 20%
dating, romance and sexuality — 6% / 17%
how to have a meaningful career — 6% / 16%
parenting — 6% / 12%
dealing with divorce — 3% / 9%
technology and digital life — 4% / 5%
none of the above — 69% / 48%

In addition to studying the opinions and perspectives of Scots, Barna assessed two groups of Scottish churches to identify best practices for thriving faith communities. "Baseline churches" represented the norm of church communities in Scotland, while "growing churches" demonstrated substantive, outside-the-norm growth. The goal was to identify what differences, if any, distinguished these two groups of churches by interviewing both church leaders and congregants.

EXPOSITORY APPROACH TO TEACHING THE BIBLE
% among growing and baseline church leaders in Scotland

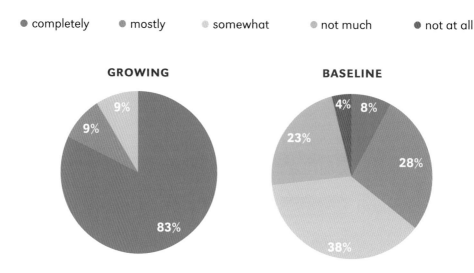

● completely   ● mostly   ● somewhat   ● not much   ● not at all

GROWING

9%
9%
83%

BASELINE

4% 8%
23%
28%
38%

Barna identified 10 characteristics of growing churches that are markedly different from baseline churches. Among these is a conscious, deliberate focus by church leaders on Bible-rich, expository preaching. Eight in 10 leaders of growing churches say it is "completely true" that their approach to teaching the Bible is expository (83%), compared to one in 12 baseline leaders (8%).

Along with a systematic approach to Bible teaching, growing church leaders (39%) are also more apt than baseline leaders (17%) to use stories and testimonies to make biblical teaching more relevant to their congregation's lives. They also more consistently marry biblical principles to life application, according to both leaders (83%, compared to 57% baseline) and the people in their congregation (62% vs. 34% baseline). These teaching strategies seem to bear fruit: More than half of people in growing churches (55%) say "the Bible teaching I receive in my church is relevant to my life"; only one-quarter of baseline churchgoers says so (27%).

ONE CHARACTERISTIC OF GROWING CHURCHES IS A CONSCIOUS, DELIBERATE FOCUS ON BIBLE-RICH, EXPOSITORY PREACHING

Teaching that is relevant and rich in biblical content also appears to foster positive outcomes in people's lives. Those in growing churches (59%) are more apt than baseline members (36%) to report that "attending church has helped me understand the Bible better." Twice as many growing church leaders (70%) as baseline leaders (33%) say "discipleship, Bible teaching and worship at our church help attenders to develop a biblical worldview."

In what areas of their lives do congregations feel the greatest impact of their church's Bible teaching? Most notably, two-thirds of people in growing churches say their church's Bible teaching and engagement has helped them grow closer to God (65%), compared with fewer than half of baseline churchgoers (45%). They are also somewhat more likely to say Bible teaching has helped them be more confident about sharing their faith (34% vs. 26%).

The apparent impact of expository Bible teaching on the growth of faith communities points to the importance of a solid biblical foundation for churches in a post-Christian context. And young Scots' interest in the Bible may signal a growing hunger for the gospel among younger generations who have had less exposure to the Church. In an ironic twist, an overall move toward a post-Christian, secularized culture may create greater interest in Christianity and offer Christians more opportunities to share their faith with a curious, receptive audience.

THE IMPACT OF EXPOSITORY BIBLE TEACHING POINTS TO THE IMPORTANCE OF A SOLID BIBLICAL FOUNDATION FOR CHURCHES IN A POST-CHRISTIAN CONTEXT

PART V

DEEPENING BIBLE ENGAGEMENT

Now that we have assembled a picture of the Bible in America, we can zoom out to determine some of the strategic implications of the research. The question at hand for Christian leaders is, *How can we deepen Bible engagement?* Barna and American Bible Society have more to learn through further research, but what we have discovered thus far has implications for prayer and action.

There are no easy answers in an era of intensifying skepticism, iterative technology, changing demographics and morals based on self-fulfillment. It is time for clear thinking and courageous leadership, especially when it comes to the Bible. Leaders must assess reality and make strategic decisions in light of those facts. To help, here are 10 insights the Barna team has culled from this work—insights to propel you to prayer and action.

1. The Bible Is Still Good News in America

Although the nation's population shows increasing signs of a post-Christian shift, more than 135 million adults are engaged with or friendly toward the Bible. A majority of adults view the Bible as sacred. It is often used as a source of guidance and tens of millions hear the voice of God through its pages. Don't underestimate the window of opportunity these findings represent. *How can we reactivate scriptural "muscle memory" so the Bible comes alive again in people's lives?*

2. Young People Must Be the Priority

Without intervention, the future of Bible engagement is less bright than the past, and there is no clearer portrait of this reality than the Millennial generation. Although Millennial Christians continue to stoke a bright flame of passion for the Scriptures, their numbers are dwindling and their non-believing and non-practicing peers have put the Bible on a dusty shelf. To generate the best long-term outcomes, consider prioritizing the youngest generations, especially children, youth and young adults. This is not to exclude efforts with older adults, but the most significant payoff will be with those under the age of 30—generally speaking, the younger the better. *How can we relieve and redirect the anti-Bible pressure on young people?*

TO GENERATE THE BEST LONG-TERM OUTCOMES, PRIORITIZE THE YOUNGEST GENERATIONS—CHILDREN, YOUTH AND YOUNG ADULTS

3. The Scriptures Can Be Trusted

One way is to help them understand the reliability of the Bible. Why can it be trusted? What is its claim on human beings today? One interesting development of the last decade is the degree to which snarky, cynical humor has made it harder to have earnest conversations about important topics like the reliability of the Scriptures. Yet we must find ways to persuade people in a distracted and cynical age that the Bible is sufficient for life. *How can we offer clear and courageous advocacy for the Bible?*

4. Bible Engagement Needs a Plan

A strategic game plan can lead to transformative change when it comes to Bible engagement. For example, we could think about the four levels of Bible engagement and deploy specific efforts to assist people engaged at each level. Even in a local church setting, the congregation is comprised of a mix of individuals from these segments. *How can we help people deepen their engagement from one category to the next?*

- Build on the strengths of the **Bible engaged**. Help them unleash their passion for the Scriptures by giving them tools to advocate for the Bible cause. Enlist them in the "campaign"; make this a mission. Equip them to deepen their relational engagement of the Bible, including within their families and with those whom they mentor.

- The **Bible friendly** segment accounts for nearly two out of five U.S. adults, and they represent an enormous strategic opportunity. They have the tools (e.g., a Bible in their home) and the motivation to read the Bible more. They need to know the Bible isn't just a place to go in times of trouble or for advice; it's a primary way to experience God. And they may need assistance to grasp the Bible's scope, history and meaning. Yet many of these individuals are only partially engaged with many elements of spirituality, including churchgoing, so the barriers to deeper engagement are often more than the Bible itself.

- **Bible neutral** adults typically turn to the Bible, if they do at all, when they need comfort. There is nothing wrong with this motivation, but it is possible to turn these moments of comfort into patterns of behavior. Given their profile of disconnection from church and ambivalence about making faith a priority, it will take significantly more effort deepen the engagement of someone in the neutral category.

- **Bible skeptics** are vital for their input, critiques and concerns. Their viewpoint ensures that Christian leaders' efforts stay connected to the reality on the ground—the cultural dialogue about Christianity and its sacred literature. The Bible may be somewhat unfamiliar to this segment, but it is accessible even to most skeptics (for example, two-thirds own a Bible).

5. The Scriptures Are for the Community

Most U.S. adults use the Bible in individual rather than communal ways, and we can help people rediscover relational Bible use.

EQUIP THE BIBLE ENGAGED TO DEEPEN THEIR RELATIONAL ENGAGEMENT OF THE BIBLE WITHIN THEIR FAMILIES AND WITH THOSE WHOM THEY MENTOR

According to Barna research in the UK, people report gleaning more wisdom from the Bible when they "discuss the Bible in a group." And one of the ways Millennials stay connected to faith is developing meaningful relationships with other Christian adults. *How can our churches facilitate social and communal forms of Bible engagement?*

6. The Bible Is a Guide for Cultural Discernment

The Bible provides the Christian community with a map for cultural discernment. Its wisdom can be the grid for understanding what is happening in society, in our communities and in our hearts. Without a biblical framework for "understanding the times and knowing what to do" (1 Chron. 12:32), Christians are too easily tossed by the cultural tides—yet the story of Daniel, for example, offers remarkably timely insights for living in a religiously pluralistic culture. *How can Christians read the Bible as a map for living faithfully in a changing world?*

7. Cultural Discernment Is a New Apologetic

Wise cultural discernment helps Christians—but what if cultural discernment could also help church outsiders, and offer evidence for the Scriptures' reliability and significance for today? In a society that is struggling with digital overload, for example, the notion of "digital Sabbath"—intentional time away from screens—is a powerful argument for the Bible's continuing relevance. When one-quarter of Millennials believes they have a decent chance of being famous by age 25, Ecclesiastes offers a bracing antidote to a fame-obsessed generation. Pick a dimension of culture—sex and sexuality, terrorism, leadership, greed, ambition—and God's word has wisdom to spare. *How can we effectively communicate the Bible's relevant-yet-countercultural ways of thinking and living?*

8. Digital Tools Are Tools, Not Magic Bullets

Many observers of the Bible landscape attest to the effectiveness of digital tools, such as YouVersion, to increase access to the Scriptures—but we must do more than provide a catalogue of available products. Leaders mentor, guide and teach others how to blend diverse resources into their Bible engagement practices. Leaders also ask younger Christians for input and guidance as they bring new practices and priorities to the table. *How can we teach people to use all the tools at their disposal to more deeply engage the Bible?*

9. The Bible Speaks to 21st-Century Vocations

People spend much of their time in careers and work environments where the Bible may seem thousands of years out of step with the times. Yet the Scriptures relate directly to what God calls 21st-century Christians to do with their lives. Sadly, only 10 percent of Catholic Millennials and 16 percent of Protestant Millennials have "learned how the Bible applies to my field or interest area." For effective Bible engagement and transformational discipleship, this must change. *How can we connect the Bible with the work of human beings?*

10. Barriers to Bible Engagement Are Spiritual

Americans continue to find ways to under-prioritize engagement with the Bible. They lack time. They are too busy. They already know what it says. Even Christian leaders sometimes find convenient excuses for not being as engaged with the Bible as they need to be. At the end of the day, each of the obstacles to deeper engagement is a spiritual barrier that needs a spiritual solution.

People need help to cultivate humble eagerness to engage God's word. They need to know the Bible is not simply solace for our human woes, but even more an experience of the living God who wants to transform lives from now to eternity—and they need the prayers of their fellow Christians and the Spirit's presence to activate that knowledge in their own lives. *How can we break down spiritual barriers to engaging with the Scriptures—even in our own hearts?*

> PEOPLE NEED TO KNOW THE BIBLE IS NOT SIMPLY SOLACE FOR OUR HUMAN WOES, BUT EVEN MORE AN EXPERIENCE OF THE LIVING GOD

★   ★   ★

As a final word of encouragement, take stock of your own context in light of the insights and conclusions found in *The Bible in America*.

What findings do you see reflected in the lives of those around you? Is your community more Bible-minded or less—and what will that mean for how you encourage deeper engagement with the Scriptures? As a nation, America is undergoing rapid cultural change. How do you see these changes at work around you, especially when it comes to the Bible?

Whatever changes are still to come, the Scriptures bear witness to God's ultimate purposes—to redeem, renew and restore his people and his world—so seismic cultural change is no cause for fear. "My word is like the snow and the rain that come down from the sky to water the earth. They make the crops grow and provide seed for planting and food to eat. So also will be the word that I speak—it will not fail to do what I plan for it; it will do everything I send it to do" (Is. 55:10–11).

WHATEVER CHANGES ARE STILL TO COME, THE SCRIPTURES BEAR WITNESS TO GOD'S ULTIMATE PURPOSES—TO REDEEM, RENEW AND RESTORE HIS PEOPLE AND HIS WORLD

A Message from Roy Peterson, President of American Bible Society

The following sentence anchors the end of an address given by Elias Boudinot when he founded American Bible Society in 1816:

We shall do our part toward that expansion and intensity of light divine, which shall visit, in its progress, the palaces of the great and the hamlets of the small, until the whole "earth be full of the knowledge of Jehovah, as the waters cover the sea"!

This inspirational sentence stayed with me as I pored over the information in this book—particularly that first phrase, "We shall do our part. . ." Given the declining trends we're seeing in both the attitudes and actions of Americans toward the Bible, what is "our part" in seeing an awakening of Bible engagement in the U.S.?

We start with complete confidence in God. No, the sky is not falling. We are not doomed to a Bible-barren future or a nation of people who have walked away from the gospel message. We still serve a sovereign God who is not surprised by any of this data, and who still calls us to do our part in the advancement of Christian love and hope. May we hear the same question that Isaiah heard from God, and may we respond the same way: "Then I heard the Lord say, 'Whom shall I send? Who will be our messenger?' I answered, 'I will go! Send me!'" (Is. 6:8).

While each of us has a different part, there are certain elements that I pray are critical to us all. First, that we are actively engaging the Scriptures ourselves, creating daily opportunities to be shaped and guided by God's word of life. Second, that we are actively involved in the local church. Third, that we pray often for the Bible cause both here in this country and around the world. As we continue to pray and engage the Bible in our community, we will become living witnesses to the power of Christ to transform the human heart.

ROY PETERSON

Roy Peterson joined American Bible Society as president and CEO in 2014. Prior to that, he spent 10 years as CEO of The Seed Company. He also held several leadership positions at Wycliffe Bible Translators, including president and CEO. Peterson received a Bachelor of Science in Business Administration before earning a Master of Arts in Leadership Studies from Azusa Pacific University. Peterson and his wife, Rita, live in Philadelphia and have four children and five grandchildren.

When it comes to Bible ministry, we live in one of the most exciting times in human history. Today, the Bible stands ready to change the world as we know it. Consider with me these three tremendous opportunities:

- *Our nation is at a crossroads:* In this season of deepening divisions across political, racial, religious and socioeconomic lines, we are witnessing an awakening across this nation to the unifying power of God's word. Today we have the opportunity to choose a path of growing Bible engagement or growing Bible skepticism. Let's choose together the path of personal increased Bible engagement so that Christ may be glorified through our lives.

- *The human heart is at a crossroads:* As wonderful as our cities are in all their vibrant and diverse potential, many are still gripped by poverty, violence, corruption and oppression. Terror, trauma and mass migrations caused by civil wars and groups like ISIS and Boko Haram seem to be ratcheting up global levels of anxiety to new heights. Communities around the world are crippled by decades of civil wars, gang wars, modern day slavery and other abuses that leave survivors devastated by trauma. But there is an awakening to the power of God's word to restore and transform the human heart. We're seeing Bible-based trauma healing ministry make tremendous impact on thousands in some of the most hostile and remote regions of the world.

- *Humanity itself is at a crossroads:* We live in a globally connected world awash in information. And yet a billion people still lack the full Bible in their heart language. Nearly a quarter of the world's active languages do not have a single word of scripture translated. But thanks to unprecedented achievements in technology and global collaboration,

WHEN IT COMES TO BIBLE MINISTRY, WE LIVE IN ONE OF THE MOST EXCITING TIMES IN HUMAN HISTORY there is an awakening to the power of God's word to reach "every tribe and every nation." Our generation could be the first since the Tower of Babel to see God's word proclaimed in every language on the planet as the final 1,800 translation projects get underway.

Whether it's skepticism in the U.S., trauma here and around the world or this landmark stage in the history of Bible translation, we are living in a critically important time for God's word around the world. And each of us has a part.

What is yours? As you consider your role in the Bible cause, I will leave you with this beautiful prayer from the Scriptures:

I ask God from the wealth of his glory to give you power through his Spirit to be strong in your inner selves, and I pray that Christ will make his home in your hearts through faith. I pray that you may have your roots and foundation in love, so that you, together with all God's people, may have the power to understand how broad and long, how high and deep, is Christ's love. Yes, may you come to know his love—although it can never be fully known—and so be completely filled with the very nature of God. To him who by means of his power working in us is able to do so much more than we can ever ask for, or even think of: to God be the glory in the church and in Christ Jesus for all time, forever and ever! Amen (Eph. 3:14–21).

WE ARE LIVING IN A CRITICALLY IMPORTANT TIME FOR GOD'S WORD AROUND THE WORLD—AND EACH OF US HAS A PART.

APPENDIX

A: DATA TABLES

The following data are from Barna's six-year aggregate database of American Bible Society's "State of the Bible" findings, unless otherwise indicated. Definitions for each of the segments included in the tables can be found in the Glossary on page 164.

1. What books, if any, do you consider sacred literature or holy books?

	% ALL U.S. ADULTS	GENDER		GENERATION				
		% MEN	% WOMEN	% TEENS	% MILLENNIALS	% GEN-XERS	% BOOMERS	% ELDERS
the Bible	81	77	85	89	71	79	87	88
the Koran	10	12	9	13	14	12	10	7
the Book of Mormon	4	4	4	11	5	5	3	3
the Torah	5	6	5	15	8	6	5	3
other	4	3	4	1	4	3	4	3
none	12	14	9	9	18	13	8	7
not sure	4	4	3		5	4	3	3

2. Which of the following do you think has had the most impact on humanity? (2016 only)

	% ALL U.S. ADULTS	GENDER		GENERATION				
		% MEN	% WOMEN	% TEENS	% MILLENNIALS	% GEN-XERS	% BOOMERS	% ELDERS
the Bible	64	60	67		51	64	69	76
On the Origin of Species	6	5	6		8	6	5	4
the Koran	6	5	2		6	7	5	4
The Republic by Plato	5	6	5		9	5	5	1
The Art of War by Sun Tzu	4	9	2		9	2	2	1
none of these	6	8	5		7	7	6	4
not sure	10	7	13		10	9	10	11

ETHNICITY			REGION				FAITH SEGMENT				
% WHITE	% BLACK	% HISPANIC	% NORTHEAST	% MIDWEST	% SOUTH	% WEST	% PRACTICING MAINLINE	% PRACTICING NON-MAINLINE	% PRACTICING CATHOLIC	% NON-PRACTICING CHRISTIAN	% NO FAITH + OTHER FAITH
82	89	79	76	82	85	75	93	96	93	91	37
11	9	8	16	11	8	12	6	4	11	11	20
5	3	3	4	3	4	7	2	1	3	4	4
6	4	4	9	7	4	7	4	2	8	5	10
3	3	4	4	4	2	6	4	1	3	2	9
12	4	12	16	12	10	17	2	2	4	5	44
3	4	6	5	3	4	4	3	1	2	3	7

ETHNICITY			REGION				FAITH SEGMENT				
% WHITE	% BLACK	% HISPANIC	% NORTHEAST	% MIDWEST	% SOUTH	% WEST	% PRACTICING MAINLINE	% PRACTICING NON-MAINLINE	% PRACTICING CATHOLIC	% NON-PRACTICING CHRISTIAN	% NO FAITH + OTHER FAITH
65	70	55	58	64	70	59	80	88	67	61	38
7	2	5	8	5	5	5	0	4	3	6	13
3	3	9	4	4	3	3	3	2	8	6	10
5	4	8	6	4	5	8	0	1	5	6	11
6	3	4	7	7	5	5	1	2	3	4	4
5	6	9	8	5	4	9	5	1	3	6	14
9	12	12	9	11	9	11	11	4	12	12	10

3. Do you agree or disagree with the following statement? The Bible contains everything a person needs to know to live a meaningful life.

		GENDER			GENERATION			
	% ALL U.S. ADULTS	% MEN	% WOMEN	% TEENS	% MILLENNIALS	% GEN-XERS	% BOOMERS	% ELDERS
strongly agree	48	43	54	41	32	46	55	61
somewhat agree	20	21	20	28	24	20	19	18
somewhat disagree	14	15	13	11	21	15	12	9
strongly disagree	15	18	12	9	19	17	12	10
don't know	2	3	2	11	3	2	3	2

4. Do you think the Bible has too much, too little or just the right amount of influence in U.S. society today?

		GENDER			GENERATION			
	% ALL U.S. ADULTS	% MEN	% WOMEN	% TEENS	% MILLENNIALS	% GEN-XERS	% BOOMERS	% ELDERS
too much	16	19	13	13	26	17	12	8
too little	51	46	55	44	35	51	57	58
just right	28	30	26	25	34	27	26	28
don't know	5	5	5	18	5	5	5	6

ETHNICITY			REGION				FAITH SEGMENT				
% WHITE	% BLACK	% HISPANIC	% NORTHEAST	% MIDWEST	% SOUTH	% WEST	% PRACTICING MAINLINE	% PRACTICING NON-MAINLINE	% PRACTICING CATHOLIC	% NON-PRACTICING CHRISTIAN	% NO FAITH + OTHER FAITH
46	69	47	33	51	61	40	71	85	57	45	7
20	16	24	26	19	17	20	17	10	22	26	15
15	8	14	19	14	11	18	5	3	13	17	23
16	6	14	20	13	11	21	5	1	6	10	49
3	2	1	2	3	1	2	2	1	2	2	5

ETHNICITY			REGION				FAITH SEGMENT				
% WHITE	% BLACK	% HISPANIC	% NORTHEAST	% MIDWEST	% SOUTH	% WEST	% PRACTICING MAINLINE	% PRACTICING NON-MAINLINE	% PRACTICING CATHOLIC	% NON-PRACTICING CHRISTIAN	% NO FAITH + OTHER FAITH
17	8	17	23	12	14	22	4	2	6	12	53
54	55	42	42	53	55	43	67	78	63	50	12
24	33	35	29	29	27	29	24	18	28	34	27
5	4	5	5	5	3	6	4	2	3	5	9

5. Does your household own a Bible?

| | % ALL U.S. ADULTS | GENDER | | GENERATION | | | | |
		% MEN	% WOMEN	% TEENS	% MILLENNIALS	% GEN-XERS	% BOOMERS	% ELDERS
yes	88	87	89	72	80	85	92	94
no	12	13	11	28	19	15	8	6

6. How often, if ever, do you actually read the Bible, not including times when you are at a church service or church event?

| | % ALL U.S. ADULTS | GENDER | | GENERATION | | | | |
		% MEN	% WOMEN	% TEENS	% MILLENNIALS	% GEN-XERS	% BOOMERS	% ELDERS
never	25	28	22	33	34	28	21	18
less than once a year	10	11	10	15	11	11	11	9
once or twice a year	10	11	9	8	12	10	10	8
three or four times a year	8	8	7	8	7	8	8	7
once a month	8	9	8	10	8	9	8	7
once a week	8	8	9	10	8	8	8	10
several times a week	9	8	10	8	6	9	10	11
four or more times a week	5	4	6	4	4	6	6	6
every day	14	11	17	4	9	10	16	23
not sure	2	2	2		1	1	2	3

	ETHNICITY			REGION				FAITH SEGMENT				
	% WHITE	% BLACK	% HISPANIC	% NORTHEAST	% MIDWEST	% SOUTH	% WEST	% PRACTICING MAINLINE	% PRACTICING NON-MAINLINE	% PRACTICING CATHOLIC	% NON-PRACTICING CHRISTIAN	% NO FAITH + OTHER FAITH
	88	95	87	83	91	92	85	99	100	96	94	61
	11	5	13	17	9	8	15	1	0	4	6	38

	ETHNICITY			REGION				FAITH SEGMENT				
	% WHITE	% BLACK	% HISPANIC	% NORTHEAST	% MIDWEST	% SOUTH	% WEST	% PRACTICING MAINLINE	% PRACTICING NON-MAINLINE	% PRACTICING CATHOLIC	% NON-PRACTICING CHRISTIAN	% NO FAITH + OTHER FAITH
	27	11	25	34	24	17	29	2	2	12	23	60
	12	6	10	12	11	7	12	4	2	11	14	13
	10	8	10	11	9	8	11	4	3	13	14	9
	8	8	8	7	7	7	7	6	3	12	11	5
	8	10	10	8	9	10	8	15	7	12	10	4
	8	10	9	8	9	9	8	19	11	13	8	2
	8	14	10	7	10	12	7	14	21	12	7	2
	5	8	4	4	6	7	5	11	14	4	3	1
	13	23	12	9	15	21	12	22	38	10	9	2
	2	3	2	1	2	1	2	1	1	2	2	2

7. Do you wish that you read the Bible more or not?

| | % ALL U.S. ADULTS | GENDER | | GENERATION | | | | |
		% MEN	% WOMEN	% TEENS	% MILLENNIALS	% GEN-XERS	% BOOMERS	% ELDERS
yes	62	57	67	62	56	61	65	64
no	36	41	32	38	43	38	33	34
don't know	2	2	2		1	2	2	2

8. I read the Bible because:

| | % ALL U.S. ADULTS | GENDER | | GENERATION | | | | |
		% MEN	% WOMEN	% TEENS	% MILLENNIALS	% GEN-XERS	% BOOMERS	% ELDERS
It brings me closer to God	57	54	61	60	50	57	60	61
I have a problem I need to solve or I need direction	16	20	13	6	21	18	16	11
I need comfort	13	11	16	8	12	13	14	15
I know I'm supposed to	5	6	4	15	5	5	4	4
It is part of my studies at school	3	4	2	4	7	2	2	3
don't know	5	7	4		5	4	5	6

| ETHNICITY | | | REGION | | | | FAITH SEGMENT | | | | |
% WHITE	% BLACK	% HISPANIC	% NORTHEAST	% MIDWEST	% SOUTH	% WEST	% PRACTICING MAINLINE	% PRACTICING NON-MAINLINE	% PRACTICING CATHOLIC	% NON-PRACTICING CHRISTIAN	% NO FAITH + OTHER FAITH
58	77	68	54	62	70	54	80	86	74	64	18
40	20	31	45	36	28	44	18	13	24	34	80
2	2	1	1	3	2	2	2	1	2	2	2

| ETHNICITY | | | REGION | | | | FAITH SEGMENT | | | | |
% WHITE	% BLACK	% HISPANIC	% NORTHEAST	% MIDWEST	% SOUTH	% WEST	% PRACTICING MAINLINE	% PRACTICING NON-MAINLINE	% PRACTICING CATHOLIC	% NON-PRACTICING CHRISTIAN	% NO FAITH + OTHER FAITH
59	61	54	55	57	61	53	61	72	60	50	24
15	15	20	18	20	14	16	14	12	17	19	18
13	13	17	15	14	12	18	14	9	15	17	5
5	6	4	4	2	6	5	4	4	3	5	10
3	2	2	3	2	3	4	3	1	2	3	22
5	3	5	3	5	4	5	4	2	3	6	21

9. These days, the Bible is available and used in different formats. Which of the following have you used within the past year?

	% ALL U.S. ADULTS	GENDER		GENERATION				
		% MEN	% WOMEN	% TEENS	% MILLENNIALS	% GEN-XERS	% BOOMERS	% ELDERS
Read from a print version of the Bible on your own	88	86	89	68	84	86	90	89
Heard the Bible read in a worship service or mass	85	83	86	87	81	81	88	90
Attended a small group or Bible study, where you studied the Bible in a group, not including weekend worship services	47	43	50	48	52	45	44	50
Used the Internet on a computer to read Bible content	42	43	41	28	57	51	38	18
Downloaded or used a Bible app on a smartphone	31	30	31	29	50	38	23	6
Searched for Bible verses or Bible content on a smartphone or cell phone	30	32	29	33	61	41	20	6
Listened to an audio version of the Bible	28	27	28	14	26	28	29	27
Listened to a teaching about the Bible via podcast	27	25	29	11	28	28	28	23

ETHNICITY			REGION				FAITH SEGMENT				
% WHITE	% BLACK	% HISPANIC	% NORTHEAST	% MIDWEST	% SOUTH	% WEST	% PRACTICING MAINLINE	% PRACTICING NON-MAINLINE	% PRACTICING CATHOLIC	% NON-PRACTICING CHRISTIAN	% NO FAITH + OTHER FAITH
89	89	81	83	87	88	84	93	94	88	84	74
86	87	80	82	85	88	80	98	94	89	77	58
44	58	48	37	47	51	43	53	67	35	34	27
41	43	42	45	43	45	43	40	50	34	36	49
27	42	36	35	26	33	28	24	44	18	27	19
26	39	38	42	30	39	35	25	38	19	27	33
24	38	31	26	24	30	29	28	39	18	22	19
24	34	30	25	26	32	30	26	36	18	23	19

10. Which of the following statements comes closest to describing what you believe about the Bible?

	% ALL U.S. ADULTS	GENDER		GENERATION				
		% MEN	% WOMEN	% TEENS	% MILLENNIALS	% GEN-XERS	% BOOMERS	% ELDERS
The Bible is the actual word of God and should be taken literally, word for word	24	20	27	22	16	22	26	31
The Bible is the inspired word of God and has no errors, although some verses are meant to be symbolic rather than literal	30	29	32	34	30	30	31	29
The Bible is the inspired word of God but has some factual or historical errors	14	15	14	14	15	15	14	12
The Bible was not inspired by God but tells how the writers of the Bible understood the ways and principles of God	9	10	9	8	11	9	9	9
The Bible is just another book of teachings written by men that contains stories and advice	16	20	12	14	23	16	13	11
other	2	2	2	9	2	2	2	3
don't know	5	4	5		4	5	4	5

| ETHNICITY | | | REGION | | | | FAITH SEGMENT | | | | |
% WHITE	% BLACK	% HISPANIC	% NORTHEAST	% MIDWEST	% SOUTH	% WEST	% PRACTICING MAINLINE	% PRACTICING NON-MAINLINE	% PRACTICING CATHOLIC	% NON-PRACTICING CHRISTIAN	% NO FAITH + OTHER FAITH
20	40	27	17	21	30	19	33	45	23	23	4
31	32	32	27	34	35	26	41	44	46	31	8
16	10	13	19	15	10	16	14	6	17	19	9
10	5	7	11	10	7	13	5	2	6	11	14
17	7	14	21	15	12	21	3	1	3	9	55
2	2	2	2	3	3	3	2	1	2	2	4
4	4	4	2	2	2	2	3	1	2	4	6

11. Bible engagement

	% ALL U.S. ADULTS	GENDER		GENERATION				
		% MEN	% WOMEN	% TEENS	% MILLENNIALS	% GEN-XERS	% BOOMERS	% ELDERS
Engaged	18	14	22	7	12	15	21	26
Friendly	38	37	39	49	36	39	39	37
Neutral	27	28	25	22	27	29	26	24
Skeptic	18	21	14	23	25	18	15	13

ETHNICITY			REGION				FAITH SEGMENT				
% WHITE	% BLACK	% HISPANIC	% NORTHEAST	% MIDWEST	% SOUTH	% WEST	% PRACTICING MAINLINE	% PRACTICING NON-MAINLINE	% PRACTICING CATHOLIC	% NON-PRACTICING CHRISTIAN	% NO FAITH + OTHER FAITH
17	29	15	12	19	26	16	30	50	13	11	2
36	46	46	34	38	41	32	48	41	59	45	10
29	17	23	30	25	18	27	19	8	23	34	29
18	9	16	24	19	15	25	4	1	5	10	59

B: PROFILES OF BIBLE ENGAGEMENT

The following pages are fact sheets about each of the four Bible-engagement groups—their beliefs, perceptions and practices, including:

- Beliefs about God

- Beliefs about Jesus' sinlessness

- Perceptions of and beliefs about the Bible

- Bible reading habits

- How the Bible influences their lives

- Faith practices such as church attendance, volunteering and charitable giving

A PROFILE OF THE BIBLE ENGAGED

A person who is "engaged" has a high view of Scripture and reads the Bible four or more times per week.

They view the Bible as 1) the actual or 2) the inspired word of God with no errors, or as 3) the inspired word of God with some errors. They must also read, use or listen to the Bible four times a week or more to be considered Engaged.

DEMOGRAPHICS

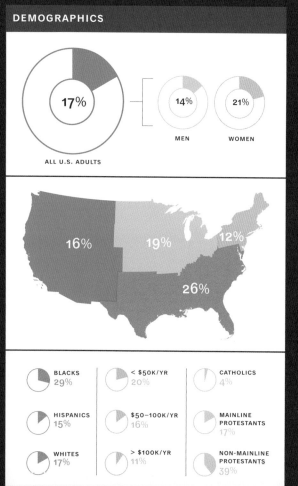

17%
ALL U.S. ADULTS

14%
MEN

21%
WOMEN

16%   19%   12%

26%

BLACKS 29%

HISPANICS 15%

WHITES 17%

< $50K/YR 20%

$50–100K/YR 16%

> $100K/YR 11%

CATHOLICS 4%

MAINLINE PROTESTANTS 17%

NON-MAINLINE PROTESTANTS 39%

BELIEFS ABOUT GOD

Bible-engaged Americans overwhelmingly hold a traditional orthodox view of God.

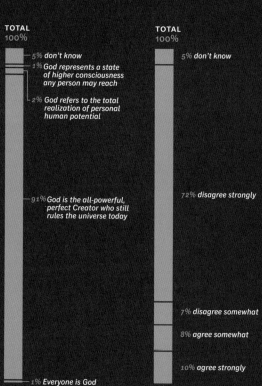

TOTAL
100%

5% don't know

1% God represents a state of higher consciousness any person may reach

2% God refers to the total realization of personal human potential

91% God is the all-powerful, perfect Creator who still rules the universe today

1% Everyone is God

BELIEFS ABOUT JESUS AND SIN

And eight out of 10 disagree with the statement, "When he lived on earth, Jesus Christ was human and committed sins like other people."

TOTAL
100%

5% don't know

72% disagree strongly

7% disagree somewhat

8% agree somewhat

10% agree strongly

READING HABITS AND BIBLE PERCEPTIONS

Bible-engaged folks read the Bible regularly yet still wish they had more time to study and meditate on the Scriptures. They see Bible reading as individually and socially beneficial, and worry about its diminished influence on society.

74%
read the Bible every day

81%
wish they read the Bible more

56%
say their Bible use increased over the past year

43%
say their top frustration when it comes to reading the Bible is not having enough time to read it

71%
give a lot of thought to how they can apply what they read in the Bible to their own life

81%
believe regular Bible reading leads to a less fearful life

75%
say the Bible has too little influence on U.S. society today

71%
are definitely concerned about the decline of Bible reading in America

THE BIBLE HAS A LOT OF INFLUENCE ON ...

Most people who are highly engaged with the Bible allow it to shape how they engage with their world, including political issues.

87% my views on abortion

63% the decisions I make about finances and money

52% my decision on who to vote for in the upcoming election

45% my support for refugees and displaced people

44% my support for wars our country fights

43% what I buy

38% my views on gun ownership

32% how I feel about immigration

26% the stores where I choose to shop

BELIEFS ABOUT THE BIBLE

The vast majority believes biblical precepts are personally fulfilling, and they hold what is traditionally known as a "high" view of the Scriptures.

85%
say the Bible contains everything a person needs to know to live a meaningful life

47%
believe it is the actual word of God

45%
believe it is the inspired word of God with no errors

FAITH PRACTICES

As you might expect, Bible-engaged Americans are much more likely than other U.S. adults to be involved in faith practices other than Bible reading. Most are regular churchgoers and many are disciplined about financial giving and acts of service.

76% **11%**
attended a worship service within the past week, 11% within the past month

36%
volunteered at a church within the past week

19%
volunteered for a nonprofit within the past week

49%
gave $2,000 or more to charity, including churches, in 2015
(The average annual donation was $1,500, compared to $200 among all U.S. adults.)

Barna / American Bible Society 2016; N=2,011. Totals may not equal 100 percent due to rounding.

A PROFILE OF THE BIBLE FRIENDLY

The "friendly" person also has a high view of Scripture, but reads it less frequently.

Like the engaged, they hold a high view of Scripture, but read or use the Bible fewer than four times in a week.

DEMOGRAPHICS

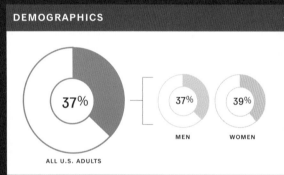

37%

37% MEN

39% WOMEN

ALL U.S. ADULTS

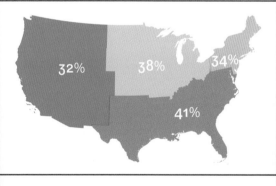

32%

38%

34%

41%

BLACKS
46%

< $50K/YR
40%

CATHOLICS
48%

HISPANICS
46%

$50–100K/YR
37%

MAINLINE PROTESTANTS
47%

WHITES
36%

> $100K/YR
32%

NON-MAINLINE PROTESTANTS
45%

BELIEFS ABOUT GOD

Most Bible-friendly Americans hold a traditional orthodox view of God.

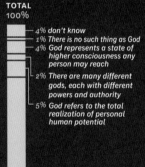

TOTAL
100%

4% don't know
1% There is no such thing as God
4% God represents a state of higher consciousness any person may reach
2% There are many different gods, each with different powers and authority
5% God refers to the total realization of personal human potential

81% God is the all-powerful, perfect Creator who still rules the universe today

4% Everyone is God

BELIEFS ABOUT JESUS AND SIN

But fewer of them are orthodox when it comes to the statement, "When he lived on earth, Jesus Christ was human and committed sins like other people."

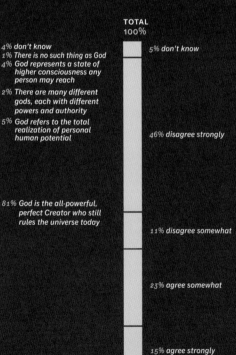

TOTAL
100%

5% don't know

46% disagree strongly

11% disagree somewhat

23% agree somewhat

15% agree strongly

READING HABITS AND BIBLE PERCEPTIONS

Bible-friendly people hold the Scriptures in high esteem but most read the Bible only on occasion. Eight in 10 wish they read it more. Many see Bible reading as individually and socially beneficial, but only three in 10 worry about its diminished influence on society.

17%
read the Bible at least once a week

14%
read it once a month

78%
wish they read the Bible more

23%
say their Bible use increased over the past year

42%
say their top frustration when it comes to reading the Bible is not having enough time to read it

49%
give a lot of thought to how they can apply what they read in the Bible to their own life

30%
believe regular Bible reading leads to a less fearful life

60%
say the Bible has too little influence on U.S. society today

29%
are definitely concerned about the decline of Bible reading in America

THE BIBLE HAS A LOT OF INFLUENCE ON ...

Perhaps because they read it so infrequently, few report that the Bible informs their everyday lives or their thinking on today's social issues.

40% my views on abortion

19% the decisions I make about finances and money

16% my support for refugees and displaced people

15% my decision on who to vote for in the upcoming election

13% my support for wars our country fights

12% how I feel about immigration

10% my views on gun ownership

8% what I buy

6% the stores where I choose to shop

BELIEFS ABOUT THE BIBLE

Nearly six in 10 believe biblical precepts are personally fulfilling, and most hold what is traditionally known as a "high" view of the Scriptures.

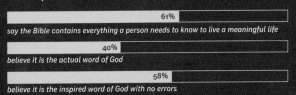

61%
say the Bible contains everything a person needs to know to live a meaningful life

40%
believe it is the actual word of God

58%
believe it is the inspired word of God with no errors

FAITH PRACTICES

Bible-friendly Americans attend church more regularly than the U.S. norm, but are half as likely as those who are Bible engaged to have served at their church during the past week. They are less likely, as well, to give regularly to a church.

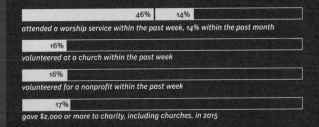

46%   14%
attended a worship service within the past week, 14% within the past month

16%
volunteered at a church within the past week

16%
volunteered for a nonprofit within the past week

17%
gave $2,000 or more to charity, including churches, in 2015

Barna / American Bible Society 2016; N=2,011. Totals may not equal 100 percent due to rounding.

A PROFILE OF THE BIBLE NEUTRAL

Someone who is "neutral" has a lower, but not negative, view of Scripture.

This person neither chooses the top two statements about the Bible (i.e., the highest views) nor the most skeptical statement about the Bible. They tend to pick the "middle options" in the survey. They rarely or never read the Bible.

DEMOGRAPHICS

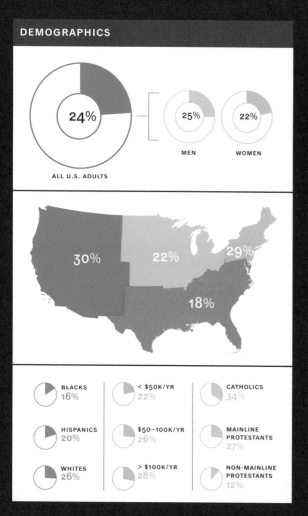

24%
ALL U.S. ADULTS

25% MEN

22% WOMEN

30% 22% 29%
18%

BLACKS 16%
HISPANICS 20%
WHITES 26%

< $50K/YR 22%
$50–100K/YR 26%
> $100K/YR 28%

CATHOLICS 34%
MAINLINE PROTESTANTS 27%
NON-MAINLINE PROTESTANTS 12%

BELIEFS ABOUT GOD

A majority of Bible-friendly Americans holds an orthodox view of God—but the other half are all over the map.

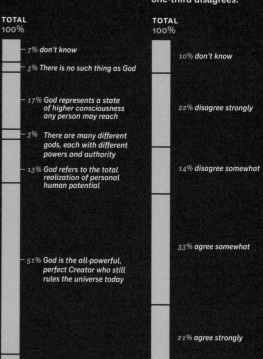

TOTAL 100%

7% don't know

3% There is no such thing as God

17% God represents a state of higher consciousness any person may reach

3% There are many different gods, each with different powers and authority

13% God refers to the total realization of personal human potential

51% God is the all-powerful, perfect Creator who still rules the universe today

6% Everyone is God

BELIEFS ABOUT JESUS AND SIN

A majority also diverges from orthodoxy when it comes to the statement, "When he lived on earth, Jesus Christ was human and committed sins like other people." Just one-third disagrees.

TOTAL 100%

10% don't know

22% disagree strongly

14% disagree somewhat

33% agree somewhat

21% agree strongly

READING HABITS AND BIBLE PERCEPTIONS

Bible-neutral people read the Scriptures about as often as Bible-friendly folks, and about half wish they read it more. They are much less likely than either Bible-engaged or Bible-friendly segments to say the Scriptures ought to have a greater role in American life.

7%
read the Bible at least once a week

9%
read it once a month

47%
wish they read the Bible more

11%
say their Bible use increased over the past year

26%
say their top frustration when it comes to reading the Bible is not having enough time to read it

18%
say it's that the language is difficult to relate to

36%
give a lot of thought to how they can apply what they read in the Bible to their own life

11%
believe regular Bible reading leads to a less fearful life

37%
say the Bible has too little influence on U.S. society today

12%
are definitely concerned about the decline of Bible reading in America

THE BIBLE HAS A LOT OF INFLUENCE ON …

Except when it comes to their views on abortion, fewer than one in 10 report that the Bible informs their lives or positions on various issues.

11% my views on abortion

8% my support for refugees and displaced people

5% the decisions I make about finances and money

5% my views on gun ownership

4% my decision on who to vote for in the upcoming election

4% my support for wars our country fights

3% how I feel about immigration

2% what I buy

2% the stores where I choose to shop

BELIEFS ABOUT THE BIBLE

Half believe the Bible is inspired by God but that it contains some historical or factual errors, and another two in five say it is the various writers' best understanding of God's ways.

23%
say the Bible contains everything a person needs to know to live a meaningful life

50%
believe it is the inspired word of God with some errors

35%
believe it tells how the writers understood the ways and principles of God

FAITH PRACTICES

One-third of those who are Bible neutral have attended church within the past week or month, and they are about as equally likely as Bible-friendly Americans to volunteer for a nonprofit or give more than $2,000 annually to charity.

25% **9%**
attended a worship service within the past week, 14% within the past month

8%
volunteered at a church within the past week

17%
volunteered for a nonprofit within the past week

18%
gave $2,000 or more to charity in 2015

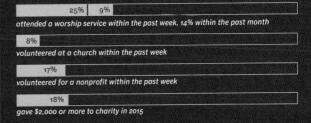

Barna / American Bible Society 2016; N=2,011. Totals may not equal 100 percent due to rounding.

A PROFILE OF THE BIBLE SKEPTIC

Someone who is a "skeptic" believes the Bible is just another book of teachings written by men.

The Bible skeptic selects the statement in the survey that reflects the lowest view of the Bible – that it is "just another book of teachings written by men." In other words, there is no God "behind" the Bible according to skeptics. They rarely or never read the Bible.

DEMOGRAPHICS

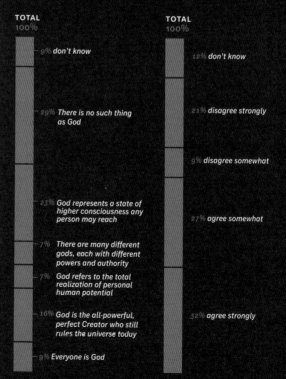

22%

ALL U.S. ADULTS

21% MEN

14% WOMEN

25%   19%   24%

15%

BLACKS 9%

HISPANICS 16%

WHITES 18%

< $50K/YR 16%

$50–100K/YR 18%

> $100K/YR 24%

CATHOLICS 14%

MAINLINE PROTESTANTS 9%

NON-MAINLINE PROTESTANTS 4%

BELIEFS ABOUT GOD

A majority of Bible skeptics believes either that there is no God or that "God" represents a state of human higher consciousness.

TOTAL 100%

- 9% don't know
- 29% There is no such thing as God
- 23% God represents a state of higher consciousness any person may reach
- 7% There are many different gods, each with different powers and authority
- 7% God refers to the total realization of personal human potential
- 16% God is the all-powerful, perfect Creator who still rules the universe today
- 9% Everyone is God

BELIEFS ABOUT JESUS AND SIN

Only three in 10 disagree with the statement, "When he lived on earth, Jesus Christ was human and committed sins like other people."

TOTAL 100%

- 12% don't know
- 21% disagree strongly
- 9% disagree somewhat
- 27% agree somewhat
- 32% agree strongly

READING HABITS AND BIBLE PERCEPTIONS

Two-thirds of Bible skeptics do not ever read the Bible, yet about one in five says they would like to read it more. Half are concerned about the Bible having too much influence on U.S. society and say they are not concerned about diminished Bible engagement in America.

62%
never read
the Bible

5%
read it once
a month or
more often

21%
wish they read
the Bible more

4%
say their
Bible use
increased over
the past year

24%
say their top
frustration when
it comes to reading
the Bible is that
they don't feel
excited to read it

46%
strongly disagree
that regular Bible
reading leads to a
less fearful life

50%
say the Bible
has too much
influence on U.S.
society today

55%
are definitely
not concerned
about the decline
of Bible reading
in America

NINE OUT OF 10 SAY THE BIBLE HAS NO INFLUENCE ON ...

Most skeptics say the Bible does not influence their views or their lives at all.

- my views on abortion
- my support for refugees and displaced people
- the decisions I make about finances and money
- my views on gun ownership
- my decision on who to vote for in the upcoming election
- my support for wars our country fights
- what I buy
- how I feel about immigration
- the stores where I choose to shop

BELIEFS ABOUT THE BIBLE

Nine out of 10 believe the Bible is merely a book of manmade teaching, and the other one in 10 categorize their beliefs as "other." Just one in nine skeptics say the Bible's contents are a comprehensive guide to a meaningful life.

11%
say the Bible contains everything a person needs to know to live a meaningful life

91%
believe the Bible is just another book of teachings written by men

FAITH PRACTICES

Perhaps surprisingly, one in 10 Bible skeptics went to church last week, and one in 20 attended in the past month. However, they are below the U.S. norm when it comes to volunteerism and philanthropy.

10% 5%
attended a worship service within the past week, 5% within the past month

1%
volunteered at a church within the past week

14%
volunteered for a nonprofit within the past week

13%
gave $2,000 or more to charity in 2015
(The average annual donation was $100, compared to $200 among all U.S. adults.)

Barna / American Bible Society 2016; N=2,011. Totals may not equal 100 percent due to rounding.

C: GLOSSARY

Theolographics

"Theolographics" are Barna's way of describing people's beliefs and practices related to faith or religion.

Practicing faith means a person identifies with a religion, says their faith is very important in their life and has attended a religious service or gathering (other than a special occasion such as a holiday, wedding or funeral) within the past month.

Practicing Christians meet the criteria for practicing faith and identify themselves as Christian (includes Catholics and Protestants).

Practicing Catholics meet the criteria for practicing faith and identify themselves as Catholic (subset of practicing Christians).

Practicing Protestants meet the criteria for practicing faith and attend a church affiliated with a Protestant denomination (subset of practicing Christians).

Bible readers read the Bible at least three to four times a year outside of a worship service, Mass or church event.

Bible-minded people believe the Bible is accurate in all the principles it teaches and have read the Scriptures within the past week.

Bible-engagement definitions are based on data collected for the American Bible Society's annual "State of the Bible" study. Barna created a four-part typology based on people's view of and level of engagement with the Scriptures.

Bible engaged means that people have a "high" view of the Scriptures and read the Bible four or more times per week. They view the Bible as a) the *actual* or b) the *inspired* word of God with no errors, or as c) the *inspired* word of God with some errors. They must also read, use or listen to the Bible four times a week or more to be considered Bible engaged.

Bible friendly people also have a "high" view of the Scriptures but read it less frequently. They are similar to the Bible engaged in their definitions of the Bible, but read it fewer than four times in a week.

Bible neutral people have a lower, but not negative, view of the Bible. This person chooses neither of the top two definitions of the Bible (i.e., the "highest" views) nor the most skeptical statement. They tend to pick "middle options" and rarely or never read the Bible.

Bible skeptics believe the Bible is just another book of teachings written by men. The Bible skeptic selects the statement in the survey that reflects the "lowest" view of the Bible and rarely or never read it.

Demographics

Generations

Millennials were born between 1984 and 2002
    (adults 18 and older only).
Gen-Xers were born between 1965 and 1983.
Boomers were born between 1946 and 1964.
Elders were born prior to 1946.
Teens were ages 13 to 17 in 2015, the year of the "State of
    the Bible: Teens" study.

Ethnicity is based on respondents' self-descriptions of their ethnicity. Those who describe themselves as Hispanic plus another ethnicity are coded as Hispanic only. To ensure adequate sample sizes, Barna usually segments the population only by the three largest ethnic groups:

> White / Caucasian
> Black / African American
> Hispanic / Latino

D: METHODOLOGY

The data reported in *The Bible in America* are based on a series of telephone and online interviews with nationwide random samples.

Dates	Audience	Collection method	Sample size	Sampling error	Funded by
2011–2016	U.S. adults	telephone and online	12,187	±0.9	American Bible Society
Jan–Feb, 2016	U.S. adults	telephone and online	2008	±2.0	American Bible Society
Feb 2015	U.S. teens 13–17	online	1,056	±2.9	American Bible Society
2006–2016	U.S. adults	telephone and phone	±1000 each	±3.0	Barna Group
2005–2015	U.S. adults	telephone and online	65,064	±0.4	Barna Group
Apr 2015	U.S. Protestant senior pastors	telephone and online: preliminary data	448	±4.5	Pepperdine University
Aug 2014	U.S. Millennials	online	1,000	±3.0	Barna, American Bible Society

All telephone interviews were conducted by Barna Group. All households were selected for inclusion in the sample using a random-digit dial technique, which allows every telephone household in the nation to have an equal and known probability of selection. Households selected for inclusion in the survey sample received multiple callbacks to increase the probability of obtaining a representative distribution of adults. Regional quotas were used to ensure that sufficient population dispersion was achieved. There were also minimum and maximum ranges placed on the distribution of respondents within several demographic variables, which were tracked during the field process to ensure that statistical weighting would not be excessive. When a particular attribute reached one of the parameters, the sampling selection process was varied to preclude individuals who did not meet the necessary demographic criterion, with the interviewer seeking a person from the same household who fit the desired criterion. Between 20 and 40 percent of telephone interviews were conducted on cell phones.

Online interviews were conducted using an online research panel called KnowledgePanel® based on probability sampling that covers both the online and offline populations in the U.S. Panel members are randomly recruited by telephone and by self-administered mail and web surveys. Households are provided with access to the Internet and hardware, if needed. Unlike other Internet research that covers only individuals with Internet access who volunteer for research, this process uses a dual sampling frame that includes both listed and unlisted phone numbers, telephone and non-telephone households, and cell-phone-only households. The panel is not limited to current Web users or computer owners. All potential panelists are randomly selected to join the KnowledgePanel; unselected volunteers are not able to join.

Once data was collected, minimal statistical weights were applied to several demographic variables to more closely correspond to known national averages.

When researchers describe the accuracy of survey results, they usually provide the estimated amount of "sampling error." This refers to the degree of possible inaccuracy that could be attributed to interviewing a group of people that is not completely representative of the population from which they were drawn. For general population surveys, see the table above for maximum sampling error.

There is a range of other errors that can influence survey results—e.g., biased question wording, question sequencing, inaccurate recording of responses, inaccurate data tabulation, etc.—errors whose influence on the findings cannot be statistically estimated. Barna Group makes every effort to overcome these possible errors at every stage of research.

E: ENDNOTES

1. For more on this idea, check out David Lomas, *The Truest Thing About You: Identity, Desire, and Why It All Matters* (Colorado Springs: David C. Cook, 2014).
2. YouVersion.com "Total Engagement to Date" streaming updates. https://www.youversion.com/happening-now (accessed April 2016).
3. See George Barna and David Kinnaman, *Churchless: Understanding Today's Unchurched and How to Connect with Them* (Carol Stream, IL: Tyndale House Publishers, 2014).
4. Doreen Carvajal, "The Bible, a Perennial Bestseller, Runs into Sales Resistance, *The New York Times*, October 28, 1996. http://www.nytimes.com/1996/10/28/business/the-bible-a-perennial-runs-into-sales-resistance.html
5. Data on teens and U.S. adults from the 2016 "State of the Bible" research and the "State of the Bible: Teens" study, N=1,039, completed in 2015; data on practicing Christians from "State of the Bible 2011–2016."
6. Barna Group, *Making Space for Millennials: A Blueprint for Your Culture, Ministry, Leadership and Facilities* (Ventura, CA: Barna Group, 2014).

ACKNOWLEDGEMENTS

Barna Group offers our heartfelt congratulations to American Bible Society on the occasion of their bicentennial, and our deepest thanks for their partnership in this crucial ongoing research. The "State of the Bible" findings are essential data for anyone seeking to further the Bible cause, and we salute their generosity in sharing this knowledge with the Church. Thanks especially to our esteemed colleagues at American Bible Society, including:

- Dr. Roy Peterson, President
- Geof Morin, Senior Vice President of Ministry Mobilization
- Jason Malec, Managing Director of Mission U.S.
- Andrew Hood, Managing Director of Communications

Barna also wishes to thank our generous contributors to *The Bible in America*, which include Claude Alexander, Bonnie Camarda, John Fea, Rob Hoskins, Mario Paredes and Randy Petersen. Your insights bring the data out of the realm of theory and into everyday life—and we are exceedingly grateful.

The research team for *The Bible in America* and the "State of the Bible" national studies is David Kinnaman, Pam Jacob, Brooke Hempell and Roxanne Stone. Joyce Chiu, Inga Dahlstadt, Katie Fitzgerald, Traci Hochmuth and Megan Pritchett also contributed analysis. Under the editorial direction of Roxanne Stone, *The Bible in America* was written by David Kinnaman, Aly Hawkins, Cory Maxwell-Coghlan and Alyce Youngblood. Cover and infographics were designed by Nathan Stock and Chaz Russo who, along with Bill Denzel, also offered creative direction to the project. Rob Williams created the charts, graphs, tables and book layout, and Brenda Usery managed production. Amy Brands and Matt Carobini provided marketing support. Cassie Bolton, Elaine Klautzsch, Jill Kinnaman and Todd White kept the Barna office, teams and projects running smoothly.

ABOUT

Barna Group is a research firm dedicated to providing action-able insights on faith and culture, with a particular focus on the Christian church. In its 30-year history, Barna Group has conducted more than one million interviews in the course of hundreds of studies, and has become a go-to source for organizations that want to better understand a complex and changing world from a faith perspective.

Barna's clients include a broad range of academic institutions, churches, non-profits, and businesses, such as Alpha, the Templeton Foundation, Pepperdine University, Fuller Seminary, the Bill and Melinda Gates Foundation, the Maclellan Foundation, DreamWorks Animation, Focus Features, Habitat for Humanity, the Navigators, NBC-Universal, the ONE Campaign, Paramount Pictures, the Salvation Army, Walden Media, Sony and World Vision.

The firm's studies are frequently quoted by major media outlets such as *The Economist*, BBC, CNN, *USA Today*, the *Wall Street Journal*, Fox News, Huffington Post, *The New York Times* and the *Los Angeles Times*.

Since 1816, American Bible Society has worked to make the Bible available to every person in a language and format each can understand and afford, so all people may experience its life-changing message. One of the nation's first and most enduring ministries, today's American Bible Society provides resources across a variety of platforms enabling first-time readers and seasoned theologians alike to engage with the bestselling book of all time. For more information, visit American.Bible.

Stay Informed About Cultural Trends

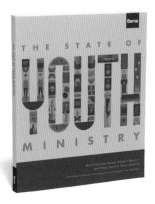

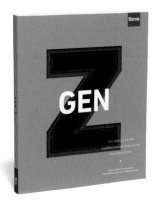

Barna Trends 2018
A beautifully designed and engaging look at today's trending topics that includes new data, analysis, infographics, and interviews right at your fingertips.

State of Youth Ministry
A wide-angle view of the youth ministry landscape that will spark conversations and lead to more effective student ministries, healthier youth workers, and sturdier teen faith.

Gen Z
Critical data to help the church effectively reach, serve and equip the emerging generation, helping them to confidently follow Jesus in today's rapidly changing culture.

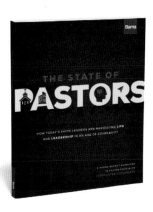

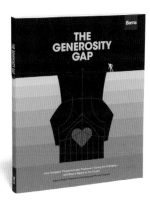

The State of Pastors
Pastoring in a complex cultural moment is not easy. Read about how church leaders are holding up in this whole-life assessment of U.S. pastors.

The Generosity Gap
Generosity is changing. Read about how pastors and laypeople perceive and practice generosity, and learn methods for strengthening giving habits.

The Porn Phenomenon
This study exposes the breadth and depth of pornography's impact and confirms that we can no longer ignore its impact on the next generation.

AVAILABLE AT BARNA.COM/RESOURCES